An Outline of English Literature

Frontispiece illustration for Daniel Defoe's Robinson Crusoe, 1719

An Outline of English Literature

NEW EDITION

G. C. Thornley and Gwyneth Roberts

Longman

Longman Group UK Limited,
Longman House, Burnt Mill, Harlow,
Essex CM20 2JE, England
and Associated Companies throughout the world.

© Longman Group Ltd 1984.

First published 1968
New edition 1984
Eighth impression 1990

ISBN 0-582-74917-4

Set in 10/12 pt Monophoto Baskerville (169)

Produced by Longman Group (FE) Ltd
Printed in Hong Kong

Acknowledgements

We should like to thank the following for permission to reproduce the photographs:

H. R. Beard Collection, Theatre Museum, Victoria and Albert Museum for page 164; The British Museum for pages 6, 9, 11, 17, 19, 51 Library for page 29; Chatto & Windus Ltd for page 152; Corpus Christi Library, Oxford for page 16; The Courtauld Institute for page 150 right; The Trustees of the Devonshire Collection, Chatsworth for page 51 left; Zoe Dominic for pages 168, 172 and 174; Fay Godwin for page 161; John Haynes for page 173; Her Majesty the Queen for page 60; The Huntingdon Library, California for page 14; Imperial War Museum for pages 184 and 185; James Joyce Museum for page 142; Kobal Collection for pages 147 and 162; MacClancy Collection for page 138; Manchester Public Libraries for the frontispiece; Mander and Mitchenson Theatre Collection for page 38; Mansell Collection for pages 22, 34 top, 62 top, 68, 74 top, 82, 83, 90, 100, 102, 116, 121, 132–3, 140; The National Gallery for page 70; The National Portrait Gallery for pages 28, 40, 98, 105, 111, 114, 180 and 182; Norwich Castle Museum for page 13; Radio Times Hulton Picture Library for pages 34 bottom, 62 bottom, 69, 80, 88, 96, 108, 134; Universal Pictorial Press for page 196; Victoria and Albert Museum for page 56; Josiah Wedgwood and Sons Ltd for page 145.

We are grateful to the following for permission to reproduce copyright material:

Jonathan Cape Ltd on behalf of the Executors of the Estate of C. Day Lewis for an extract from poem 'Carol' by C. Day Lewis from *Collected Poems 1954* pubd. The Hogarth Press; Faber & Faber Ltd for extracts from poems 'September 1st, 1939' by W.H. Auden from *The English Auden*, 'Embassy' & 'Lullaby' ('Lay your sleeping Head') by W.H. Auden from *Collected Poems 1909–1962*, 'Whatever you Say, Say Nothing' by Seamus Heaney from *North* and 'Hawk Roosting' by Ted Hughes from *Lupercal*; the Author, Roy Fuller for an extract from his poem 'War Poet' from *Collected Poems 1936–1961* pubd. Andre Deutsch Ltd; Granada Publishing Ltd for extract from poem 'Dark Well' by R.S. Thomas from *Tares* pubd. Grafton Books. A division of the Collins Pubg. Group; Authors' agents on behalf of the Estate of Robert Graves for an extract from 'She tells her love while half asleep' by Robert Graves from *Collected Poems 1975*; The Marvell Press for extract from poem 'Coming' by Philip Larkin from *The Less Deceived*; George Sassoon for an extract from poem 'The glory of Women' by Siegfried Sassoon from *Collected Poems* pubd. Faber & Faber Ltd, 1956; James McGibbon as Stevie Smith's Literary Executor for extract from her poem 'Not Waving but Drowning' from *The Collected Poems of Stevie Smith* (Penguin Modern Classics); Authors' agents for extracts from poems 'Do not go gentle into that good night' & 'In my craft or sullen art' by Dylan Thomas from *The Poems* pubd. J.M. Dent; Authors' agents on behalf of Michael B. Yeats & Macmillan London Ltd for extracts from poems 'An Irish Airman Foresees his Death' & 'The Circus Animal's Desertion' by W.B. Yeats from *The Collected Poems of W.B. Yeats*.

Contents

Saint Mark, a detail from the Lindisfarne Gospels written and illustrated around A.D. 700. These, like much of the writing of that time, were written by monks in Latin. (A Gospel is a holy book.)

Chapter One

Old English literature

The Old English language, also called Anglo-Saxon, was the earliest form of English. It is difficult to give exact dates for the rise and development of a language, because it does not change suddenly; but perhaps it is true to say that Old English was spoken from about A.D. 600 to about 1100.

The greatest Old English poem is *Beowulf*, which belongs to the seventh century. It is a story of about 3,000 lines, and it is the first English epic.[1] The name of its author is unknown.

Beowulf is not about England, but about Hrothgar, King of the Danes, and about a brave young man, Beowulf, from southern Sweden, who goes to help him. Hrothgar is in trouble. His great hall, called Heorot, is visited at night by a terrible creature, Grendel, which lives in a lake and comes to kill and eat Hrothgar's men. One night Beowulf waits secretly for this thing, attacks it, and in a fierce fight pulls its arm off. It manages to reach the lake again, but dies there. Then its mother comes to the hall in search of revenge, and the attacks begin again. Beowulf follows her to the bottom of the lake and kills her there.

In later days Beowulf, now king of his people, has to defend his country against a fire-breathing creature. He kills the animal but is badly wounded in the fight, and dies. The poem ends with a sorrowful description of Beowulf's funeral fire. Here are a few lines of it, put into modern letters:

---

[1] *epic*, the story in poetry of the adventures of a brave man (or men)

alegdon tha tomiddes   maerne theoden
haeleth hiofende   hlaford leofne
ongunnon tha on beorge   bael-fyra maest
wigend weccan   wudu-rec astah
sweart ofer swiothole   swogende leg
wope bewunden.
The sorrowing soldiers then laid the glorious prince, their dear lord,
in the middle. Then on the hill the war-men began to light the
greatest of funeral fires. The wood-smoke rose black above the
flames, the noisy fire, mixed with sorrowful cries.

The old language cannot be read now except by those who have made a special study of it. Among the critics who cannot read Old English there are some who are unkind to the poem, but *Beowulf* has its own value. It gives us an interesting picture of life in those old days. It tells us of fierce fights and brave deeds, of the speeches of the leader and the sufferings of his men. It describes their life in the hall, the terrible creatures that they had to fight, and their ships and travels. They had a hard life on land and sea. They did not enjoy it much, but they bore it well.

The few lines of *Beowulf* given above do not explain much about this kind of verse, and it may be well to say something about it. Each half-line has two main beats. There is no rhyme.[2] Instead, each half-line is joined to the other by alliteration[3] *(middes/maerne; haeleth/hiofende/hlaford; beorge/bael; wigend/weccan/wudu; sweart/ swiothole/swogende)*. Things are described indirectly and in combinations of words. A ship is not only a ship: it is a sea-goer, a sea-boat, a sea-wood, or a wave-floater. A sailor is a sea-traveller, a seaman, a sea-soldier. Even the sea itself *(sae)* may be called the waves, or the sea-streams, or the ocean-way. Often several of these words are used at the same time. Therefore, if the poet wants to say that the ship sailed away, he may say that the ship, the sea-goer, the wave-floater,

---

[2] *rhyme*, ending two or more verse lines with the same sounds. Two lines *rhyme* when each has the same vowel sound bearing the last stress (beat) – e.g. *pay* and *day* or *pay* and *weigh* as last words. Any sounds after that vowel are exactly the same – e.g. *meeting* and *beating;* but the sound before that vowel is different – e.g. *state* and *weight* are rhymes but *meet* and *meat* are not true rhymes.

[3] *alliteration*, two or more words beginning with the same sound.

A page from Beowulf including the lines given here in the text.

set out, started its journey and set forth over the sea, over the ocean-streams, over the waves. This changes a plain statement into something more colourful, but such descriptions take a lot of time, and the action moves slowly. In Old English poetry, descriptions of sad events or cruel situations are commoner and in better writing than those of happiness.

There are many other Old English poems. Among them are *Genesis A* and *Genesis B*. The second of these, which is short, is concerned with the beginning of the world and the fall of the angels[4]. It is a good piece of writing; the poet has thoroughly enjoyed describing God's punishment of Satan and the place of punishment for evil in Hell.[5] Most of the long *Genesis A*, on the other hand, is dull, and little more than old history taken from the Bible and put into poor Old English verse. Other poems taken straight from the Bible are the well-written *Exodus*, which describes how the Israelites left Egypt, and *Daniel*. Another poem, *Christ and Satan*, deals with events in Christ's life. There is a good deal of repetition in this work.

We know the names of two Old English poets, CAEDMON and CYNEWULF. Almost nothing now remains which is certainly Caedmon's work. He was a poor countryman who used to stay apart when his fellows sang songs to God; for Caedmon was un-educated and could not sing. One night an angel appeared to him in a dream and told him to sing God's praise. When he woke, he was able to sing, and part of one of his songs remains.

Cynewulf almost certainly wrote four poems, *Juliana, The Fates of the Apostles*,[6] *Christ*, and *Elene*. The last of these seems to have been written just before Cynewulf's death; for he says in it, 'Now are my days in their appointed time gone away. My life-joys have dis-appeared, as water runs away.' Cynewulf's poems are religious, and were probably written in the second half of the eighth century.

Other Old English poems are *Andreas* and *Guthlac*. The second of these is in two parts, and may have been written by two men. Guthlac was a holy man who was tempted in the desert. Another of

---

[4] *angel*, a servant of God in Heaven. According to old accounts, *Satan* and other angels disobeyed God and became the Devil and the Devil's servants in Hell.
[5] *hell*, the place for punishment for evil.
[6] *Apostle*, one of the twelve men chosen by Christ to preach to others.

Part of a ninth-century Anglo-Saxon manuscript, showing Jerusalem

the better poems is *The Dream of the Rood* (the rood is Christ's cross.) This is among the best of all Old English poems.

Old English lyrics[7] include *Deor's Complaint, The Husband's Message, The Wanderer* and *The Wife's Complaint.* Deor is a singer who has lost his lord's favour. So he complains, but tries to comfort himself by remembering other sorrows of the world. Of each one he says 'That passed over; this may do so also.'

There are many other poems in Old English. One of the better ones is a late poem called *The Battle of Maldon.* This battle was fought against the Danes in 991 and probably the poem was written soon after that. It has been highly praised for the words of courage which the leader uses:

> hige sceal the heardra   heorte the cenre
> mod sceal the mare   the ure maegen lytlath
> her lith ure ealdor   eall forheawen
> god on greote   a maeg gnornian
> se the nu fram this wigplegan wendan thenceth.
> *The mind must be the firmer, the heart must be the braver, the courage must be the greater, as our strength grows less. Here lies our lord all cut to pieces, the good man on the ground. If anyone thinks now to turn away from this war-play, may he be unhappy for ever after.*

In general it is fairly safe to say that Old English prose[8] came later than Old English verse; but there was some early prose. The oldest *Laws* were written at the beginning of the seventh century. Some of these are interesting. If you split a man's ear, you had to pay 30 shillings. These *Laws* were not literature, and better sentences were written towards the end of the seventh century.

The most interesting piece of prose is the *Anglo-Saxon Chronicle,* an early history of the country. There are, in fact, several chronicles, belonging to different cities. No doubt KING ALFRED (849-901) had a great influence on this work. He probably brought the different writings into some kind of order. He also translated a number of

[7] *lyric,* a poem – originally one meant to be sung – which expresses the poet's thoughts and feelings.
[8] *prose,* the ordinary written language, not specially controlled like verse.

Latin books into Old English, so that his people could read them. He brought back learning to England and improved the education of his people.

Another important writer of prose was AELFRIC. His works, such as the *Homilies*[9] (990-4) and *Lives of Saints*[10] (993-6), were mostly religious. He wrote out in Old English the meaning of the first seven books of the Bible. His prose style[11] is the best in Old English, and he uses alliteration to join his sentences together.

A model of a late Saxon village

[9] *Homily,* religious talk.
[10] *Saint,* holy man.
[11] *style,* manner of writing; one writer's special way of using language.

William Caxton, who lived from 1422 to 1491, offering a book from his press at Westminster to a lady.

Chapter Two

Middle English literature

The English which was used from about 1100 to about 1500 is called Middle English, and the greatest poet of the time was GEOFFREY CHAUCER. He is often called the father of English poetry, although, as we know, there were many English poets before him. As we should expect, the language had changed a great deal in the seven hundred years since the time of *Beowulf* and it is much easier to read Chaucer than to read anything written in Old English. Here are the opening lines of *The Canterbury Tales*[1] (about 1387), his greatest work:

> Whan that Aprille with his shoures swote
> The droghte of Marche hath perced to the rote
> *When April with his sweet showers has struck to the roots the*
> *dryness of March . . .*

There are five main beats in each line, and the reader will notice that rhyme has taken the place of Old English alliteration. Chaucer was a well-educated man who read Latin, and studied French and Italian poetry; but he was not interested only in books. He travelled and made good use of his eyes; and the people whom he describes are just like living people.

The Canterbury Tales total altogether about 17,000 lines – about half of Chaucer's literary production. A party of pilgrims[2] agree to

[1] *tale*, story.
[2] *pilgrim*, a person making a journey for religious reasons to a holy place.

An illustration from the opening of William Langland's Piers Plowman showing Piers Plowman dreaming

tell stories to pass the time on their journey from London to Canterbury with its great church and the grave of Thomas à Becket. There are more than twenty of these stories, mostly in verse, and in the stories we get to know the pilgrims themselves. Most of them, like the merchant, the lawyer, the cook, the sailor, the ploughman, and the miller, are ordinary people, but each of them can be recognized as a real person with his or her own character. One of the most enjoyable characters, for example, is the Wife of Bath. By the time she tells her story we know her as a woman of very strong opinions who believes firmly in marriage (she has had five husbands, one after the other) and equally firmly in the need to manage husbands strictly. In her story one of King Arthur's knights[3] must give within a year the correct answer to the question 'What do women love most?' in order to save his life. An ugly old witch[4] knows the answer ('To rule') and agrees to tell him if he marries her. At last he agrees, and at the marriage she becomes young again and beautiful.

Of Chaucer's other poems, the most important are probably

[3] *knight*, a man who – historically as a good fighter and leader in war – has the rank shown by the word *Sir* before his name.

[4] *witch*, a woman with unnatural (more than human) powers.

*An early illustration of
a party of pilgrims
leaving Canterbury*

Troylus and Cryseyde (1372-7?), and *The Legend*[5] *of Good Women* (1385). The former of these is about the love of the two young people. Shakespeare later wrote a play on the same subject, but his Cressida is less attractive than Chaucer's.

The old alliterative line was still in use in Chaucer's time, though not by him. *The Vision*[6] *of Piers the Ploughman*, mostly by WILLIAM LANGLAND, is a poem in this verse. It was written by a poor man to describe the sorrows of the poor. It looks a lot older than Chaucer's rhymed verse, though the two men lived at the same time. Langland sadly tells, as in a dream, how most people prefer the false treasures of this world to the true treasures of heaven. The characters in the poem are not as real as Chaucer's.

The alliterative metre[7] was used in several other poems, including *Sir Gawain and the Green Knight* (1360?), one of the stories of King Arthur and his Knights of the Round Table. Like others of these

[5] *legend*, story (usually one which has come down to us from ancient times so that we cannot be sure of the truth – adj. *legendary*).
[6] *vision*, something seen in the imagination as if in a dream; *a vision* is often a sight of things in the future.
[7] *metre*, the number and kinds of feet in the lines of poetry.

legendary stories, it tells of the adventures of one of King Arthur's knights (in this case Sir Gawain) in a struggle against an enemy with magic[8] powers as well as great strength and cunning. Sir Gawain finishes the adventure with all honour.

Perhaps the author of *Gawain* also wrote *Pearl* and *Patience,* two of the best alliterative poems of the time. Pearl was the name of the poet's daughter, who died at the age of two; but he is comforted when, in a dream, he sees her in heaven. *Patience* is the story of Jonah, who was thrown into the sea and swallowed by an immense creature of the sea, which carried him to the place where God wished him to go.

A good deal of Middle English prose is religious. The *Ancren Riwle* teaches proper rules of life for anchoresses (religious women) – how they ought to dress, what work they may do, when they ought not to speak, and so on. It was probably written in the thirteenth century. Another work, *The Form of Perfect Living,* was written by RICHARD ROLLE with the same sort of aim. His prose style has been highly praised, and his work is important in the history of our prose.

JOHN WYCLIFFE, a priest, attacked many of the religious ideas of his time. He was at Oxford, but had to leave because his attacks on the Church could no longer be borne. One of his beliefs was that anyone who wanted to read the Bible ought to be allowed to do so; but how could this be done by uneducated people when the Bible was in Latin? Some parts had indeed been put into Old English long ago, but Wycliffe arranged the production of the whole Bible in English. He himself translated part of it. There were two translations (1382 and 1388), of which the second is the better.

It is surprising that Wycliffe was not burnt alive for his attacks on religious practices. After he was dead and buried, his bones were dug up again and thrown into a stream which flows into the River Avon (which itself flows into the River Severn):

> The Avon to the Severn runs,
>   The Severn to the sea,
> And Wycliffe's dust shall spread abroad,
>   Wide as the waters be.

[8] *magic,* having the help of spirits or other more than human abilities to influence events.

Detail from the opening of Book 6 from the 1585 edition of Malory's Morte D'Arthur

An important Middle English prose work, *Morte D'Arthur* [= Arthur's Death], was written by SIR THOMAS MALORY. Even for the violent years just before and during the Wars of the Roses, Malory was a violent character. He was several times in prison, and it has been suggested that he wrote at least part of *Morte D'Arthur* there to pass the time.

Malory wrote eight separate tales of King Arthur and his knights but when Caxton [9] printed the book in 1485 (after Malory's death) he joined them into one long story. Caxton's was the only copy of Malory's work that we had until, quite recently (1933-4), a hand-written copy of it was found in Winchester College.

The stories of Arthur and his knights have attracted many British and other writers. Arthur is a shadowy figure of the past, but probably really lived. Many tales gathered round him and his knights. One of the main subjects was the search for the cup used by Christ at the Last Supper. (This cup is known as The Holy Grail.) Another subject was Arthur's battles against his enemies, including the Romans. Malory's fine prose can tell a direct story well, but can also express deep feelings in musical sentences. Here is part of the book in modern form. King Arthur is badly wounded:

> Then Sir Bedivere took the king on his back and so went with him to the water's edge. And when they were there, close by the bank, there came a little ship with many beautiful ladies in it; and among them all there was a queen. And they all had black head-dresses, and all wept and cried when they saw King Arthur.

[9] *William Caxton* (1422?-91) set up the first English printing press in 1476-7. He printed not only the works of other writers but also books from other countries translated by himself into excellent English prose.

The first English plays told religious stories and were performed in or near the churches. Many events of religious history were suitable subjects for drama.[10] These early plays, called Miracle[11] or Mystery Plays, are in four main groups, according to the city where they were acted: Chester, Coventry, York and Wakefield.

The subjects of the Miracle Plays are various: the disobedience of Adam and Eve; Noah and the great flood; Abraham and Isaac; events in the life of Christ; and so on. They were acted by people of the town on a kind of stage on wheels called a pageant. This was moved to different parts of the town, so that a play shown in one place could then be shown in another. Often several Miracle Plays were being performed at the same time in different places. Here is a short bit of *Noah's Flood* in the Chester Plays:

GOD: Seven days are yet coming
For you to gather and bring
Those after my liking
When mankind I annoy.
Forty days and forty nights
Rain shall fall for their unrights[A]
And those I have made through my mights[B]
Now think I to destroy.

NOAH: Lord, at your bidding[C] I am true
Since grace is only in you,
As you ask I will do.
For gracious[D] I you find.

[A] wrongdoing   [B] wonderful powers   [C] orders   [D] kind

Although the Miracles were serious and religious in intention, English comedy[12] was born in them. There was a natural tendency for the characters in the play to become recognizably human in their behaviour. However serious the main story might be, neither actors nor audience could resist the temptation to enjoy the pos-

[10] *drama*, stage plays; the writing of plays; adj. *dramatic*.
[11] *miracle*, an event produced by more than human powers.
[12] *comedy*, amusing plays; *a comedy* is a play meant more to entertain than to teach, usually one with a happy ending.

sibilities of a situation such as that in which Noah's wife needs a great deal of persuasion to make her go on board the ark.[13]

Other plays, in some respects not very different from the Miracles, were the Morality Plays. The characters in these were not people (such as Adam and Eve or Noah); they were virtues (such as Truth) or bad qualities (such as Greed or Revenge) which walked and talked. For this reason we find these plays duller today, but this does not mean that the original audiences found them dull. The plays presented moral truths in a new and effective way.

One of the best-known fifteenth-century Moralities is *Everyman*, which was translated from the Dutch. It is the story of the end of Everyman's life, when Death calls him away from the world. Among the characters are Beauty, Knowledge, Strength, and Good Deeds. When Everyman has to go to face Death, all his friends leave him except Good Deeds, who says finely:

> Everyman, I will go with thee and be thy guide,
> In thy most need to be by thy side.

Another kind of play, the Interlude, was common in the fifteenth and sixteenth centuries. The origin of this name is uncertain; perhaps the Interludes were played between the acts of long Moralities; perhaps in the middle of meals; or perhaps the name means a play by two or three performers. They are often funny, and were performed away from churches, in colleges or rich men's houses or gardens. One of them is *The Four P's*. In one part of this play, a prize is offered for the greatest lie; and it is won by a man who says that he never saw and never knew any woman out of patience.

The writers of these early plays are unknown until we come to the beginning of the sixteenth century. JOHN HEYWOOD wrote *The Four P's* (printed about 1545) and *The Play of the Weather* (1533), in which Jupiter, the King of the Gods, asks various people what kind of weather ought to be supplied. Heywood wrote other Interludes and was alive in Shakespeare's time.

---

[13] *Noah's Ark*, the great ship built by Noah to save two of each of God's creatures during the flood.

THE
FAERIE QVEEN:
THE
Shepheards Calendar:

Together.
WITH THE OTHER
Works of England's Arch-Poët,
EDM. SPENSER:

¶ *Collected into one Volume, and carefully corrected.*

Printed by *H. L.* for *Mathew Lownes.*
Anno Dom. **1611.**

NON TIBI

The title page of Spenser's The Faerie Queene from the 1611 edition

Chapter Three

Elizabethan poetry and prose

Many imitators of Chaucer appeared after his death in 1400, but few are of great interest. More than a century had to pass before any further important English poetry was written. Queen Elizabeth ruled from 1558 to 1603, but the great Elizabethan literary age is not considered as beginning until 1579. Before that year two poets wrote works of value.

SIR THOMAS WYATT and the EARL OF SURREY are often mentioned together, but there are many differences in their work. Both wrote sonnets,[1] which they learned to do from the Italians; but it was Wyatt who first brought the sonnet to England. Surrey's work is also important because he wrote the first blank[2] verse in English.

In the form of the sonnet Wyatt mainly followed the Italian poet Petrarch (1304-74). In this form, the 14 lines rhyme abbaabba (8) + 2 or 3 rhymes in the last six lines. The sonnets of Shakespeare are not of this form; they rhyme ababcdcdefefgg.

Wyatt has left us some good lyrics. Here is part of a lover's prayer to his girl:

---

[1] *sonnet*, a 14-line lyric poem of fixed form and rhyme pattern.

[2] *blank verse*, verse without rhymes, usually in lines of five iambic feet (each | ˘ ¯ |), e.g.

O goōd | ŏld mān! | hŏw wĕll | ĭn thēe[A] | ăppēars |
Thĕ cōn -| stănt[B]sĕr | vĭce ōf | thĕ ān | tĭque[C]wōrld |
SHAKESPEARE, *As You Like It*

[A] you   [B] never changing   [C] old

> And wilt thou leave me thus
> That hath loved thee so long
> In wealth and woe[A] among;
> And is thy heart so strong
> As for to leave me thus?
> Say nay[B]! Say nay!
>
> [A] sorrow   [B] no

Surrey's blank verse, which has been mentioned, is fairly good; he keeps it alive by changing the positions of the main beats in the lines. Marlowe's famous 'mighty[3] line' is blank verse and much finer poetry, and Shakespeare improved on it. Milton made blank verse the regular metre of epic.

Before and during the Elizabethan age, the writing of poetry was part of the education of a gentleman, and the books of sonnets and lyrics that appeared contained work by numbers of different writers. A good example of these books is Tottel's *Songs and Sonnets* (1557), which contained 40 poems by Surrey and 96 by Wyatt. There were 135 by other authors[4]. Did these popular sonnets and lyrics express real feelings, or were they just poetic exercises? Some may be of one sort and some of the other. They differ a good deal. Some contain rather childish ideas, as when a man is murdered by love and his blood reddens the girl's lips. Some are very fine indeed.

One of the best sonnets of the time was by MICHAEL DRAYTON. It begins like this:

> Since there's no help, come let us kiss and part:
> Nay[A], I have done; you get no more of me;
> And I am glad, – yea[B] glad with all my heart
> That thus so cleanly I myself can free.
>
> [A] no [B] yes

The sonnets of Shakespeare, printed in 1609, were probably written between 1593 and 1600. For whom, or to whom, did he write them? Many of them refer to a young man of good family, and may be addressed to William Herbert (the Earl of Pembroke), or the Earl of

[3] *mighty*, of great power.
[4] *author*, writer.

Southampton. At the beginning of the 1609 collection, it is said that they are for 'Mr. W. H.' Other people mentioned in the sonnets are a girl, a rival poet, and a dark-eyed beauty. Here is one of Shakespeare's sonnets:

> Who will believe my verse in time to come,
> If it were filled with your most high deserts[A]?
> Though yet, Heaven knows, it is but[B] as a tomb[C]
> Which hides your life, and shows not half your parts.
> If I could write the beauty of your eyes,
> And in fresh numbers[D] number all your graces
> The age to come would say, 'This poet lies,
> Such heavenly touches ne'er touched earthly faces.'
> So should my papers, yellowed with their age,
> Be scorned like old men of less truth than tongue;
> And your true rights be termed[E] a poet's rage[F]
> And stretched metre of an antique[G] song.
> But were some child of yours alive that time
> You should live twice – in it, and in my rhyme.
>
> [A] what you deserve [B] only [C] grave [D] verses [E] called [F] madness [G] old

The poet who introduced the Elizabethan age proper was EDMUND SPENSER. In 1579 he produced *The Shepherd's Calendar*, a poem in twelve books, one for each month of the year. Spenser was no doubt making experiments in metre and form, examining his own abilities. The poems are unequal, but those for April and November are good. They take the form of discussions between shepherds[5], and are therefore pastorals[6] – the best pastorals written in English up to that time. There are various subjects: praise of Queen Elizabeth, discussions about religion, the sad death of a girl, and so on. The nation welcomed the book; it was expecting a great literary age, and accepted this work as its beginning.

Spenser's greatest work, *The Faerie Queene* (1589-96), was planned in twelve books, but he wrote little more than the first six. The

---

[5] *shepherd*, a man who looks after sheep in the fields and open country.
[6] *pastoral*, concerning the life of shepherds (usually shepherds in an imaginary Golden Age living a simple, healthy and contented life in the open air).

'Queene' is either Queen Elizabeth or Glory as a person. There are twelve knights representing different virtues, and King Arthur is gentlemanliness. The knights' adventures are the basis for an allegory[7], but this is not clear. The greatness of the work is not in its thought or in its story. It is in the magic feeling in the air, the wonderful music of the verse, the beauty of the sound. Few people now read the whole thing; perhaps too much sweetness at once is more than the mind and spirit can bear.

Spenser invented a special metre for *The Faerie Queene*. The verse has nine lines; of these the last has six feet, the others five. The rhyme plan is ababbcbcc. This verse, the 'Spenserian Stanza'[8], is justly famous and has often been used since. Here is an example:

> Long thus she travelèd through deserts wide,
> By which she thought her wand'ring knight should pass,
> Yet never show of living wight[A] espied[B];
> Till that at length[C] she found the trodden[D] grass
> In which the track of people's footing was,
> Under the steep foot of a mountain hoar[E];
> The same she follows, till at last she has
> A damsel[F] spied[G] slow-footing her before,
> That on her shoulders sad a pot of water bore.
>
> [A] person   [B] saw   [C] at last   [D] pressed down by feet   [E] old and grey
> [F] girl   [G] seen

Spenser married Elizabeth Boyle in 1594 when he was over forty. The joy that he felt is expressed in *Epithalamion* (1595), an almost perfect marriage song. His *Prothalamion* (1596), written in honour of the double marriage of the daughters of the Earl of Worcester, contains the repeated line, 'Sweet Thames run softly till I end my song'. Spenser also wrote 88 sonnets which were published in 1595 – with the *Epithalamion* – under the title, *Amoretti*.

The Elizabethan age produced a surprising flow of lyrics. Lyric poetry gives expression to the poet's own thoughts and feelings, and for this reason we tend to picture the lyric poet as a rather

---

[7] *allegory*, a story which teaches a lesson because the people and places in it stand for other ideas. (An example is Bunyan's *Pilgrim's Progress* – see page 67).

[8] *stanza*, a group of verse lines which rhyme in a particular pattern.

dreamy unpractical person with his thoughts turned inwards. As a description of the Elizabethan lyric poets, nothing could be further from the truth. We know few details of Spenser's life, but his friend SIR PHILIP SIDNEY was a true Elizabethan gentleman of many activities – courtier, statesman, poet, soldier. It is probably true that this man, accepted as the pattern of nobility in his time, refused a cup of water when he lay dying on the battlefield of Zutphen, saying that it should be given to a wounded soldier lying near to him. Sidney's book of sonnets, *Astrophel and Stella*, was printed in 1591 after his death. Most of the poems of another great Elizabethan, SIR WALTER RALEIGH, soldier, sailor, explorer, courtier, and writer, have been lost, but the short pieces which remain show a real gift for poetic expression.

Some of the best lyrics of the time were in the dramatic works. Characters on the stage were given songs to sing to please the audience and to give some relief when necessary. In Shakespeare's *Twelfth Night*, for example, there is a very sweet lyric: (see page 44)

O mistress mine, where are you roaming?

Shakespeare's longer poems, *Venus and Adonis* and *Lucrece,* are both on the subject of love. The former of these was probably his first published[9] work. In both poems there is a kind of coldness, as if Shakespeare was only writing according to the rules, but without much feeling.

CHRISTOPHER MARLOWE, the famous dramatist, was also a fine lyric writer. *The Passionate*[10] *Shepherd to his Love* (published in 1599) starts like this:

Come live with me and be my love,
And we will all the pleasures prove
That hills and valleys, dales[A] and fields
Woods or steepy mountain yield.

[A] river-valleys

Sir Walter Raleigh wrote another poem as the girl's answer:

[9]*publish,* to print and sell (a book) to the public.
[10]*passionate,* very loving; filled with strong feeling.

*Sir Walter
Raleigh*

If all the world and love were young
And truth in every shepherd's tongue,
These pretty pleasures might me move
To live with thee and be thy love.

As the songs and sonnets of the great Elizabethan age passed slowly
away, the immense lyrical tide began gradually to lose its force.
The age that followed, the Jacobean age, was less fresh – more
interested in the mind than in heart or eye. A group of poets,
known as the Metaphysical[11] Poets, wrote verse which was generally
less beautiful and less musical, and which contained tricks of style
and unusual images[12] to attract attention. These poets mixed strong
feelings with reason, and the mixture is strange.

JOHN DONNE is the greatest metaphysical poet but it is difficult
to find a complete poem by him which is faultless. He wrote many

[11] *metaphysical* (as applied to poetry), showing clever tricks of style
and unlikely comparisons.
[12] *image*, a picture in the imagination; a writer uses *imagery* – produces in
the reader's mind images or pictures of things, actions, etc., which may be
compared with the things or ideas with which he is concerned – for certain
effects, e.g. to give life and strength to a description.

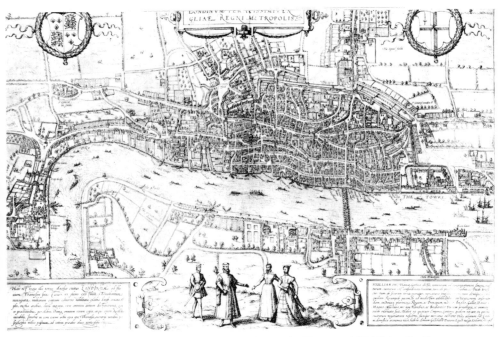

An old map of Elizabethan London on which is seen the Tower and Old Saint Paul's

good things, but no perfect poem. His songs and sonnets are probably his finest work, but he is best studied in collections of verse by various poets. He wrote a lot of poor verse which these collections omit.

Donne was a lawyer and a priest, and he wrote religious poetry, though it is not his best. In metre Donne often put the main beat on words of little importance; yet he had his good qualities. Some of his beginnings, such as 'Go and catch a falling star,' are fine. He can say effective things in a few words: 'I am two fools, I know; For loving and for saying so.' Yet some of his lines are terribly bad:

> Here lies a she sun and a he moon there
> She gives the best light to his sphere[A]
> Or each is both, and all, and so
> They unto one another nothing owe.
>
> [A] ball like the moon

The dramatist BEN JONSON, known as 'Rare Ben Jonson', was a quarrelsome man, but fearless and honest. He has left plays, poems and prose. One of his best lyrics is *To Celia*:

Drink to me only with thine eyes,
And I will pledge[A] with mine;
Or leave a kiss but in the cup,
And I'll not look for wine.

[A] drink to your health

It is time now to turn to the prose of this age, which took several very different forms. The translation of Plutarch's *Lives of the Noble Grecians and Romans* (1579), SIR THOMAS NORTH is important. It is on the whole written in fine and noble English, and it had a wide influence on Elizabethan prose. It was used by Shakespeare as a storehouse of learning. Shakespeare used quite extensive expressions from it in *Julius Caesar*, *Coriolanus* and *Antony and Cleopatra*. North was one of the best translators, with a good command of English words and the ability to weave them into powerful sentences. He did not translate directly from the Greek, but from a French translation by Amyot of Auxerre.

In 1589 RICHARD HAKLUYT collected and published *The Principal Navigations*[13], *Voyages, and Discoveries of the English Nation*. At this time there was a great deal of travel and adventure on the sea, and this book was enlarged in 1598, 1599 and 1600. It includes accounts of the voyages of the Cabots, Hawkins, Drake, and Frobisher, besides several others. Hakluyt left a lot of unpublished papers, and some of these came into the possession of Purchas.

SAMUEL PURCHAS published the Hakluyt papers under the title, *Purchas his Pilgrims* (1625), containing 'A History of the World in Sea Voyages and Land Travel'. This book deals with voyages to India, Japan, China, Africa, the West Indies and other places. Two other books by Purchas have titles which are almost the same, *Purchas his Pilgrimage, or Relations of the World and the Religions Observed in All Ages* (1613) and *Purchas his Pilgrim, or The History of Man* (1619). Another important history book of this time was Holinshed's *Chronicles*[14] (1577). Though it is known by his name, several writers were responsible for the material in it.

A kind of novel[15] began in the Elizabethan age; Lyly's *Euphues*

[13] *navigation*, finding the way in a ship from one place to another.
[14] *chronicle*, history.
[15] *novel*, a book-length single story whose characters are usually imaginary.

(1578 and 1580) started a fashion which spread in books and conversation.

JOHN LYLY was employed at court. *Euphues* has a thin love story, which is used for the purpose of giving Lyly's ideas in various talks and letters. The style is filled with tricks and alliteration; the sentences are long and complicated; and large numbers of similes[16] are brought in. A short example of this style is, 'They are commonly soonest believed that are best beloved, and they liked best whom we have known longest.' The reader forgets the thought behind the words, and looks for the machine-like arrangement of the sentences. This kind of style was common in the conversation of ladies of the time, and most of those at court were at one time Lyly's pupils. Queen Elizabeth herself used it. Every girl of good family in those days learnt to speak, not only French, but also Euphuism. Even Shakespeare was influenced by this artificial style.

Another novelist was ROBERT GREENE, whose story *Pandosto* gave Shakespeare the plot of his play *The Winter's Tale*. Another, THOMAS NASH, a writer of very independent character, refused to copy Euphues or anyone else. His book *The Life of Jacke Wilton* was a picaresque novel, that is to say, a novel of adventure about men of bad character. Picaresque novels were first written in Spain and then copied elsewhere. The interest of the adventure is sometimes spoilt by long speeches which are made just when we want the speaker to do something instead of talking.

These Elizabethan 'novels' are of little value on the whole, and few people read them now. They did not lead on to the great novels of later years. They were a false start, and died out.

The prose of FRANCIS BACON is important. His *Essays*[17] especially are popular still. They first appeared in 1597 and then with additions in 1612 and 1625. The sentences in the earlier essays are short, sharp and effective; the style of the later essays is rather more flowing. Some of the best-known sayings in English come from Bacon's books, and especially from the *Essays*.

---

[16] *simile,* the use of an image – usually introduced by *like* or *as* – to make a comparison in one respect with the thing or idea described (e.g. 'the elephant looked as big *as a house*').

[17] *essay,* a composition of moderate length on a general subject; usually a number of the writer's personal ideas on the subject, and not a complete examination of the matter.

Here are a few, with the title of the essay:

> Men fear death as children fear to go in the dark. *(Death)*
> All colours will agree in the dark. *(Unity in Religion)*
> Revenge is a kind of wild justice. *(Revenge)*
> Why should I be angry with a man for loving himself better than me? *(Revenge)*
> Children sweeten labours[18] but they make misfortunes more bitter. *(Parents and Children)*
> If a man be gracious to strangers, it shows he is a citizen of the world. *(Goodness)*
> The remedy is worse than the disease. *(Troubles)*
> Stay a little, that we may make an end the sooner. *(Despatch)*
> Cure the disease and kill the patient.[19] *(Friendship)*
> That is the best part of beauty which a picture cannot express. *(Beauty)*
> Some books are to be read only in parts; others to be read, but not curiously; and some few to be read wholly. *(Studies)*
> A wise man will make more opportunities than he finds. *(Ceremonies and Respects)*

Other books by Bacon include *A History of Henry VII* (1622), which was written in a few months. *The Advancement of Learning* (1605) considers the different ways of advancing knowledge, and the divisions of knowledge, such as poetry and history. *The New Atlantis* (1626) contains social ideas in the form of a story. This story is of a journey to an imaginary island, Bensalem, in the Pacific Ocean. Bacon wrote several other books in English and Latin.

The Authorized[20] Version[21] (A.V.) of the Bible appeared in 1611. The history of the English Bible is important. In Old English several translations of *parts* of the Bible were made, but the first complete translation was Wycliffe's. WILLIAM TYNDALE translated the New Testament from the Greek, and part of the Old Testament

---

[18] *labour*, hard work.
[19] *patient*, a person receiving treatment for an illness.
[20] *authorized*, having the support and agreement of the person or people with the power to order or forbid something.
[21] *version*, a book translated from another language (especially one of several different translations).

from the Hebrew. He was later burnt to death for his beliefs, but he is remembered for his careful and important work on the translation. The Authorized Version depended a great deal on Tyndale's work. Several other translations were made in the sixteenth century, including a complete Bible (1535) by Miles Coverdale.

A meeting was held in 1604 to consider a new translation. Forty-seven translators were appointed, and they worked in groups on different parts of the Bible. The work was finished in 1611 and the result, depending chiefly on Wycliffe and Tyndale, was called the *Authorized Version*, though in fact no one authorized it.

The language is beautiful, strong and pure, very unlike Euphuism. Most English writers are influenced in some way or other by the words of the A.V.

Here are a few sentences from *Ecclesiastes*, Chapter 12:

> Remember now thy Creator[A] in the days of thy youth, while the evil days come not, nor the years draw nigh[B] when thou shalt say, I have no pleasure in them; while the sun, or the light, or the moon, or the stars, be not darkened, nor the clouds return after the rain.
>
> [A] maker   [B] near

Timber or *Discoveries* (1640) by the dramatist Ben Jonson, is a collection of notes and ideas on various subjects. Until Jonson wrote this book, nothing had appeared to make clear the true work of a critic, his aims and limitations. Jonson says that a critic ought to judge a work as a whole, and that the critic himself must have some poetic abilities. Jonson is the father of English literary criticism. His critical ideas are not limited to this book, but appear elsewhere. He has some interesting things to say. He thought that Donne, 'for not keeping of accent [proper beat], deserved hanging'. He was not pleased with the Spenserian stanza or with Spenser's language. When he was told that Shakespeare had never 'blotted a line' (=crossed a line out), he wished that he had 'blotted a thousand'. Jonson's ideas were much influenced by the classics,[22] and this explains much of what he says.

[22] *classics*, the work of the great writers of the past.

*The inside of
an Elizabethan theatre,
the Swan Theatre in
London, 1596*

*The Globe Theatre in
Southwark where many
of Shakespeare's plays
were produced*

Chapter Four

Elizabethan drama

The chief literary glory of the great Elizabethan age was its drama, but even before it began several plays appeared which showed that a great development had taken place. They are not very good plays, but in general the comedies are better than the tragedies.[1]

The first regular English comedy was *Ralph Roister Doister* (1553?) by NICHOLAS UDALL, headmaster of Westminster School, who probably wrote it for his boys to act. It is in rough verse and contains the sort of humour[2] that may be found among country people. Another comedy was *Gammer Gurton's Needle*, acted at Cambridge University in 1566, also in rough verse. It is about the loss and the finding of a needle with which Gammer Gurton mends clothes. Quarrels, broken heads, and a drinking song are important parts of it.

Lyly's prose comedy *Campaspe* and his allegorical play *Endimion* are an improvement on this. They were performed in front of Queen Elizabeth, probably by boy actors. These boys, known as 'Children of Paul's', no doubt caused a lot of fun when they played the parts of great men such as Alexander the Great, or the philosopher,[3] Diogenes.

---

[1] *tragedy*, a very sad event (adj. *tragic*); *a tragedy* is a play with an unhappy ending, usually written in fine language and concerned with the fate of great men.

[2] *humour*, the way of seeing things which, when expressed in words or actions, makes other people smile or laugh.

[3] *philosopher*, a man learned in *philosophy*, the study of reason and of the causes and real nature of things and events.

The play *Campaspe* contains the charming (and now famous) song:

> Cupid[A] and my Campaspe played
> At cards for kisses; Cupid paid.
>
> [A] God of Love

Cupid loses one thing after another to Campaspe, and at last he offers his eyes:

> At last he set her both his eyes;
> She won, and Cupid blind did rise.
>   O Love, has she done this to thee?
>   What shall, alas![A], become of[B] me?
>
> [A] how sad!   [B] happen to

The first regular English tragedy was *Gorboduc*, in blank verse, performed in 1564. The first three acts were written by THOMAS NORTON, the other two by THOMAS SACKVILLE. It is very dull, and is about King Gorboduc of England and his family. (This man appears in Spenser's *Faerie Queene* as Gorbogud.) The blank verse is poor stuff, and nothing is *done* on the stage except some movements in silence. The story of the play is *told*.

The Spanish Tragedy (1592) by THOMAS KYD is an example of the tragedy of blood, popular at the time. Blood and death play a large part in such plays. *The Spanish Tragedy* is in some ways rather like Shakespeare's *Hamlet*. A ghost [4] appears, demanding revenge; but it appears to the father of a murdered son, not to the son of a murdered father, as in *Hamlet*. A girl who is mad, and a man with the name *Horatio* (as in *Hamlet*) also appear in the play. There is a belief that Kyd once wrote a play based on the *Hamlet* story, and that Shakespeare saw it; but it has never been found.

The first great dramatist of the time was CHRISTOPHER MARLOWE. His first tragedy, *Tamburlaine the Great* (1587 or earlier), is in two parts. It is written in the splendid blank verse that Marlowe brought to the stage. The first part deals with the rise to power of Tambur-

---

[4] *ghost,* a dead person's spirit appearing to men's sight (and hearing).

laine, a shepherd and a robber. His terrible ambition drives him ever onwards to more power and more cruelty. His armies conquer Bajazet, ruler of Turkey, whom Tamburlaine takes from place to place in a cage, like a wild animal. In the second part Tamburlaine is pulled to Babylon in a carriage. It is drawn by two kings, whom he whips and curses when they do not go fast enough. He shouts angrily:

What! Can ye draw but[A] twenty miles a day?
[A] only

When they get tired, they are taken away to be hanged, and then two spare kings have to pull the carriage. Tamburlaine drives on to Babylon, and on arrival gives orders for all the people there to be drowned. His life is violent in other ways. He cuts an arm to show his son that a wound is unimportant. He shouts for a map. 'Give me a map', he cries, 'then let me see how much is left for me to conquer all the world.'

The play was well received, but the violence of the language and of the action, and the terrible cruelty, are serious faults. Yet Marlowe's 'mighty line' fills the heart and satisfies the sense of beauty. It is usually powerful and effective, and it is not used only to describe violence. Marlowe discovered the splendid power of the sound of proper names:

Is it not brave[A] to be a king, TECHELLES,
USUMCASANE and THERIDAMAS?
Is it not passing[B] brave to be a king,
AND RIDE IN TRIUMPH[C] THROUGH PERSEPOLIS?
[A] fine [B] very [C] victory

The *Jew of Malta* (1589?) is again often violent. In it the governor of Malta taxes the Jews there, but Barabas, a rich Jew, refuses to pay. His money and house are therefore taken from him and in revenge he begins a life of violence. He poisons his own daughter, Abigail, and causes her lover to die too. He helps the Turks when they attack Malta, and so they make him governor; but he decides to kill all the Turkish officers. He arranges that the floor of a big

The title page of Marlowe's Doctor Faustus showing Faustus being tempted by the Devil

room can be made to fall suddenly, and then invites them to a meal in it. He hopes thus to destroy them while they are eating, but an enemy makes his secret known, and he himself is thrown down below the floor into a vessel of boiling water. His last words are:

Die, life! Fly, soul! Tongue, curse thy fill and die!

The language of *The Jew of Malta* is not always so fierce; sometimes the beauty of sound and rhythm [5] (and again of proper names) is very fine:

> I hope my ships
> I sent for Egypt and the bordering isles
> Are gotten up by Nilus wandering banks;
> Mine argosies[A] from Alexandria
> Loaden with spice[B] and silks, now under sail,
> Are smoothly gliding[C] down by Candy[D] shore
> To Malta through our Mediterranean Sea.
>
> [A] big ships   [B] plant with sharp taste   [C] move smoothly   [D] Crete

The softness of the last line suggests very well the quiet movement of a sailing ship in the old days.

[5] *rhythm*, the 'beat' of English verse – the way the words or parts of words pronounced with greater or slighter stress (force) follow each other to make a regular pattern of sound.

Dr. Faustus was probably acted in 1588. The play is based on the well-known story of a man (Faustus) who sold his soul to the devil so as to have power and riches in this life. Marlowe's Faustus agrees to give his soul to the devil, Mephistopheles, in return for twenty-four years of splendid life. During these years the devil must serve him and give him what he wants. The end of the play, when death is near and Faustus is filled with fear, is a highlight of terrible description.

One of the things that Faustus orders the devil to do for him is to bring back from the dead the beautiful Helen of Troy, the cause of the Trojan war. When Faustus sees her, his delight escapes from his lips in these words:

> Was this the face that launched[A] a thousand ships
> And burnt the topless towers of Ilium[B]?
> Sweet Helen, make me immortal[C] with a kiss. *(Kisses her.)*
> Her lips suck forth my soul; see where it flies!
> Come, Helen, come! Give me my soul again ...
> O, thou art fairer than the evening air,
> Clad[D] in the beauty of a thousand stars.
>
> [A] sent forth   [B] Troy   [C] undying   [D] clothed

Such beautiful language is very different from the rough verse of *Gorboduc*.

Marlowe's *Edward the Second* (1593), perhaps his best play, deals with English history. It is possible that he helped Shakespeare with the writing of parts of *Henry the Sixth* and other early plays. Certainly Marlowe's writing set an example for other dramatists in the great Elizabethan age in two important ways: the use of powerful blank verse lines to strengthen the drama, and the development of character to heighten the sense of tragedy. When Shakespeare added to these his own mastery of plot [6] and his human sympathy, the drama reached its greatest heights.

Marlowe was killed in a quarrel at a Thames-side inn before he was thirty years of age. If he had lived longer, he would probably have written other splendid plays. Shakespeare certainly thought so.

[6] *plot*, plan of a story or play – the choice and use of events for that story.

A picture of William Shakespeare from the title page of an early edition of his plays published in 1623

The order in which the plays of WILLIAM SHAKESPEARE were written is uncertain. In fact, we know very little about his life. He was born and educated at Stratford-on-Avon, married Anne Hathaway in 1582, and later went to London, where he worked in a theatre. It is known that he was an actor and dramatist by 1592.

Shakespeare's earliest work is probably seen in certain historical plays. Perhaps he began his work as a dramatist by improving the work of other writers; the three plays which tell the story of *Henry the Sixth* may be an example of this. In *Richard the Third* (1593?) and the later *Richard the Second* (1595?) we see Shakespeare gradually discovering his powers and mastering his art. In the smooth blank verse of *Richard the Third*, the sense usually ends with the line:

Oh, I have passed a miserable night,
So full of ugly sights, of ghastly[A] dreams,
That, as I am a Christian faithful man,
I would not spend another such a night
Though 't were to buy a world of happy days.

[A] terrible

In *Richard the Second* there is rather more freedom. Although the line usually ends at a natural pause, there are times when the sense pushes through from one line to the next:

For God's sake, let us sit upon the ground
And tell sad stories of the death of kings ...
All murdered; for within the hollow crown
That rounds[A] the mortal[B] temples[C] of a king
Keeps Death his court

[A] surrounds   [B] having only a man's life   [C] side of the head

The rhythm of the blank verse is still quite strictly observed; Shakespeare has not yet developed the master's freedom which brings such freshness and power to his later verse plays; but the start is here.

Romeo and Juliet (1594-5) is the first of Shakespeare's great tragedies. The plot of this story of pure and tragic love is known in all parts of the civilized world. The deaths of Romeo and Juliet are necessary: their families are enemies, and death is the only way out of their hopeless situation. The tragedy is deeply sad and moving, but without the shock of the terrible tragedies that followed later.

The first of the comedies was probably *A Comedy of Errors* (1592-3?); its plot depends on the likeness of twins[7] and the likeness of their twin servants, with the resulting confusion. The order of the early comedies after this may be *The Taming of the Shrew*[8], *The Two Gentlemen of Verona*, and *Love's Labour's Lost*. The real step forward comes with *A Midsummer Night's Dream* (1595-6), which shows Shakespeare's growing power in comedy. The different stories of

[7] *twins*, two children born at the same time to the same parents.

[8] *shrew*, noisy and troublesome woman.

this light-hearted play are mixed together with great skill. The feelings of the lovers are never allowed to tire the audience; something really funny always interrupts them in time. But there is true sympathy in the treatment of character, and a great deal of beauty in many descriptive lines.

The next play we should notice is *The Merchant of Venice* (1596-7). In this, Antonio, a merchant, borrows money from Shylock to help his friend Bassanio, who wants to marry the rich and beautiful Portia. Shylock hates Antonio and only agrees to lend the money on condition that, if it is not repaid at the right time, Antonio shall pay a pound of his flesh. When Antonio's ships are wrecked, and to everyone's surprise he cannot pay the money, Shylock demands his pound of flesh. The case is taken to court, and Antonio has no hope. Then suddenly Portia, dressed as a lawyer, appears in court. At first she tries to persuade Shylock to have mercy, but she does not succeed, even with the famous speech about mercy:

> It [mercy] droppeth as the gentle rain from heaven
> Upon the place beneath; it is twice blessed:
> It blesseth him that gives and him that takes
> 'T is mightiest in the mightiest; it becomes[A]
> The throned monarch[B] better than his crown.
>
> [A] suits   [B] king

Then Portia herself becomes hard: Shylock may have his flesh – but not one drop of blood; there is nothing about blood in the agreement. As Shylock cannot take the flesh without spilling some blood, Antonio is saved.

The story is nonsense – no one believes that living flesh can form part of an agreement at law – but the play is great. It is called a comedy, though Shylock is, in fact, badly treated. He has been called the first great Shakespearian character, the first great tragic figure.

As You Like It (1599?), another important comedy, is the story of a good duke [9] living in the forest of Arden because his evil brother has driven him out of his country. Love affairs play an important

---

[9] *duke*, a nobleman of high rank; in old plays, etc., the ruler of a country. His wife is a duchess.

part, and the interest is increased when the girl Rosalind dresses herself as a man. (No actresses appeared on the Elizabethan stage. The parts of girls were taken by men, and so 'Rosalind' was more accustomed to a man's clothes than a woman's.) Minor characters in the play include the sad and thoughtful Jacques and the wise fool Touchstone. The pastoral setting gives us some beautiful descriptions, but there is a reality about the characters that was not to be seen in earlier pastoral poetry and plays. It is true that nature at its most cruel is seen as kinder than men in courts and towns:

> Blow, blow, thou winter wind,
> Thou art[A] not so unkind
> As man's ingratitude[B]
>
> [A] you are   [B] showing that he is not grateful; unthankfulness

But Touchstone is not persuaded:

> Ay, now am I in Arden; the more fool I. When I was at home,
> I was in a better place; but travellers must be content.

Much Ado About Nothing (1598-9), a well-balanced comedy with good speeches, is also built on love affairs; yet there is a dark side of the play which is there but almost hidden. The appearance of a selfish young man who brings sorrow to others is repeated in the even darker comedy, *All's Well that Ends Well*, the date of which is uncertain.

Twelfth Night (1600?) has been called the perfection of English comedy. The whole play is alive with humour and action. The skill in the changes from bright to dark, from gentle to severe, is matched by the skill in the arrangement of the verse and prose. The Duke Orsino believes that he is in love with the Lady Olivia, but he is more in love with love. 'If music be the food of love,' he says at the beginning of the play, 'play on.' There are twins again, and they cause confusion when the girl dresses like her brother. Two knights, Sir Toby Belch and Sir Andrew Aguecheek, provide amusement with their foolish plans and their drinking. The play contains several songs. Here is one:

O, mistress mine, where are you roaming[A]?
O, stay and hear; your true love's coming,
   That can sing both high and low.
Trip[B] no further, pretty sweeting;
Journeys end in lovers meeting,
   Every wise man's son doth know.

What is love? 'T is not hereafter;
Present mirth[C] hath present laughter;
   What's to come is still unsure.
In delay there lies no plenty;
Then come kiss me, sweet and twenty,
   Youth's a stuff will not endure[D].

[A] wandering [B] dance [C] amusement [D] last

The two parts of *King Henry the Fourth* (1597-8) introduced the fat knight Sir John Falstaff to the world. Probably his importance in the play is greater than Shakespeare at first intended; but he grew to like the man, and so did his audiences, although Falstaff is certainly not a model of knighthood. The young Prince Henry (later to become King Henry the Fifth) wastes hours drinking and joking with Falstaff, who is proudly penniless, delightfully rude, fatly wicked, wonderfully unpleasant to look at, boastfully late for battles, and a cheerful coward who carries a bottle even on the battlefield. When Henry becomes king, Falstaff expects to be given a position of honour (and an endless supply of refreshment) by his old companion. What a shock he gets! 'I know thee not, old man,' is King Henry's answer to his greeting. 'Fall to thy prayers.' Much has been written about the cruel treatment of Falstaff; but Henry, as king, cannot have the fat old knight as a companion. Falstaff is heart-broken. Henry allows him some money, but considers the affairs of England more important than the affairs of Sir John Falstaff.

Henry the Fifth was performed in 1599. It is filled with the love of country and the spirit of war. Those who wanted to see Falstaff again were disappointed: he is not there. It is said that Queen Elizabeth, speaking for her people, demanded another play which would show Falstaff in love; and that Shakespeare therefore wrote

The Merry Wives of Windsor (1601?) in two weeks. It is a pleasant play, but without great importance.

It is convenient now to consider the three Roman tragedies, and then the four great tragedies. *Julius Caesar* (1599?) is probably the best Shakespearian play to read first. In the earliest plays there is not enough thought to fill the language; the later plays are difficult because so much thought is pressed into the language that it is not very clear. In *Julius Caesar* the thought and the language are about balanced. Its structure[10] is also clear: the rise from the introduction to the crisis[11] (the killing of Caesar) in Act III, and the gradual fall to the tragic end of the play (the deaths of the conspirators[12]). Further, *Julius Caesar* is not so dark and heavy as *Coriolanus*, nor so loose as *Antony and Cleopatra*.

The hero[13] is Brutus, who joins Cassius and the other conspirators in the plan to kill Caesar. They believe that he wants to make himself king. Much of the play is now famous. Before a large crowd of Roman citizens Antony makes his great speech over the body of Caesar. It begins:

> Friends, Romans, countrymen, lend me your ears!
> I come to bury Caesar, not to praise him.
> The evil that men do lives after them;
> The good is oft interred[A] with their bones.
> So let it be with Caesar ...
> [A] buried

Yet this speech is not a great deal finer than many others. On seeing the dead body of Brutus at the end of the play, his enemy Antony says:

[10] *structure*, the way something (a play) is built; when we consider the *plot* (see page 39), we are interested in the actions and events, but in discussing *structure* we are looking at the effect of the chosen arrangement on the thoughts and feelings of the audience or reader.

[11] *crisis*, the turning point in a play, when the effect on the feelings of the audience is strongest.

[12] *conspirator*, a person who has joined in a plan to harm or kill a ruler or great man.

[13] *hero*, the character (man) in a story or book who has the special sympathy of the reader or audience; *heroine*, the woman character who has such sympathy.

This was the noblest Roman of them all
All the conspirators, save[A] only he,
Did that[B] they did in envy of great Caesar.
He only, in a general honest thought,
And common good to all, made[C] one of them.
His life was gentle; and the elements[D]
So mixed in him that Nature might stand up
And say to all the world, 'This was a man!'

[A] except [B] what [C] became [D] qualities

The main subject of *Antony and Cleopatra* (1606-7) is Antony's love for the Egyptian queen. He returns to Rome from Egypt to meet Octavius Caesar, whose sister, Octavia, he marries. Cleopatra is jealous, and Antony returns to Egypt. Octavius follows with ships and men, and defeats Antony at Alexandria. Hearing (falsely) that Cleopatra is dead, Antony falls on his sword, is carried to Cleopatra, and dies in her arms. She then takes her own life by allowing a snake to bite her.

Coriolanus (1607) concerns the life and death of Caius Marcius Coriolanus, a proud Roman commander who leads his armies against the Volscians and beats them. On his return to Rome, he wishes to become one of the consuls (rulers) of the city; but to succeed in this aim, he must ask the people for votes. His pride makes this impossible: he *cannot* beg for votes or for anything else. He is driven from Rome for insulting the people, comes back with a Volscian army to attack his own city, is met there by his wife and his mother, and is persuaded to lead the army away. The Volscians then kill him for failing in his duty to them.

In each of these tragedies, the fatal weakness of character, and the tragic course of events, which together lead a great man to ruin, are clear enough. Brutus is not a practical man. He loves Rome more than he loves his friend, Caesar; but he is thrown into a situation where he must deal with practical life and war. He makes several bad mistakes. For example, he allows Antony to speak to the people *after* himself; and the crowd remembers Antony's speech better because it is later. A practical man would speak last to an uneducated crowd. He uses *reasons* to show the crowd that the murder was necessary. Antony more wisely stirs up their *feelings*.

In the next play Antony is ruined because of his love of comfort and love. Coriolanus is ruined by his terrible pride. If he had humbly asked for votes, the people would gladly have chosen him as consul; but he scorns their dirty bodies and their stupid minds. This wrecks his own life. Many men are not practical; many men love comfort; many men are proud. But they escape destruction because the course of events helps to hide their weaknesses.

In *Hamlet* (1600-1), the prince of that name suspects that his dead father, King of Denmark, has been murdered by his uncle, Claudius. Claudius has become king and has married Hamlet's mother. The ghost of Hamlet's dead father appears to him in the castle of Elsinore and tells him about the murder. Hamlet decides on revenge; but then he begins to think too much, and to hesitate. Was the ghost telling the truth? Hamlet must try to find proof of the murder. In the crisis in Act III, Hamlet has his proof. But still he hesitates. The play still holds our attention, and Hamlet keeps our sympathy, but the end is certain and unavoidable.

Hamlet's tragic weakness is hesitation, inability to act when action is needed. He is too much of a thinker.

In *King Lear* (1606?) we see an old king thrown out of his home by two wicked daughters, and treated so badly that he goes mad and dies. It is perhaps Shakespeare's greatest work, reaching into the deepest places of the human spirit; but as a play on the stage it is very difficult, if not impossible, to act. Lear's weakness is his open-ness to flattery.[14] He gives his kingdom to the two evil daughters who flatter him, and nothing to the youngest girl, who tells the truth but loves him best.

In *Macbeth* (1605-6) the hero, Macbeth, must be considered together with his wife, Lady Macbeth. Three old witches tell Macbeth that he will receive high honours and then become king. The high honours come, and he decides to help fate to make him king. King Duncan stays with him at his castle, and he and Lady Macbeth murder the King; but Duncan's sons, Malcolm and Donalbain, escape. Malcolm brings an army against Macbeth, who is killed. Lady Macbeth is already dead. Here are some words of Macbeth when he hears of her death:

---

[14] *flatter*, (n. *flattery*), to praise insincerely.

She should have died hereafter[A];
There would have been a time for such a word.
Tomorrow and tomorrow and tomorrow
Creeps in this petty pace[B] from day to day
To the last syllable[C] of recorded time;
And all our yesterdays have lighted fools
The way to dusty death. Out, out, brief candle[D]!
Life's but a walking shadow, a poor player,
That struts and frets[E] his hour upon the stage
And then is heard no more; it is a tale
Told by an idiot[F], full of sound and fury,[G]
Signifying[H] nothing.

[A] After this [B] slow speed [C] part of a word [D] short life
[E] walks proudly and worries [F] fool [G] anger [H] meaning

Compare these lines with the lines on p. 41 from *Richard the Third*.
The *Macbeth* speech has the ring of power, but the metre is treated
with the freedom of a master, and the sense runs frequently past the
end of a line.

| ĭt ĭs | ă tāle |

| Tōld | bў ăn ĭd | ĭŏt, fūll | ŏf sōund | and fūrў |

Othello (1604-5) is the story of a brave Moorish commander in
Cyprus who has a beautiful wife, Desdemona. Iago, an evil old
soldier, has seen Cassio raised in rank above him, and tries to make
Othello believe that Cassio and Desdemona are lovers. Othello too
easily believes this, and kills Desdemona. Some critics have said that
Othello has no fatal weakness; but such unquestioning jealousy is
great weakness, even if it comes from a mind too noble to doubt
evil suggestions.

The main last plays of Shakespeare are usually called the
romances. They are *Cymbeline* (1609-10), *The Winter's Tale* (1610-11),
and *The Tempest*[15] (1611-12). It is generally agreed that *The Tempest*
is his last complete play. All these works are coloured with the idea
of forgiveness. There is still wickedness in these worlds, but it is not

[15] *tempest*, storm.

the final word of the plays. Gone is the violence of the great tragedies. Instead we have happier things – beautiful islands and beautiful girls: Imogen in *Cymbeline*, Perdita in *The Winter's Tale*, and Miranda in *The Tempest*. A speech in the last of these plays seems to show that Shakespeare had decided to write no more. This is part of it:

> Our revels^A now are ended. These our actors
> As I foretold^B you, were all spirits and
> Are melted into air, into thin air . .
> We are such stuff
> As dreams are made on,^C and our little life
> Is rounded with a sleep.
>
> ^A amusements   ^B told (you) to expect   ^C of

The immense power and variety of Shakespeare's work have led to the idea that one man cannot have written it all; yet it must be true that one man did. There is usually more in the language of the later plays than at first meets the eye. They must be read again and again if we want to reach down to the bottom of the sense. If a new play is found and supposed to be by Shakespeare, we can decide whether it belongs to his later work. If it does, no one will understand the *whole* meaning at a first reading.

A great dramatist who followed Shakespeare, but who was far below him, was BENJAMIN JONSON. His work is more learned and less inspired[16] than Shakespeare's, and the ancient classics had a great influence on it. His best known play is *Every Man in his Humour* (1598). A 'humour' meant a quality made into a person, a special foolishness, or the chief strong feeling in a man. This is one of Jonson's weaknesses as a dramatist. His characters are walking humours, and not really human. In this play Kitely, a merchant, has a pretty wife and his humour is jealousy. He suspects a young man, Knowell, of having ideas about the pretty wife. Knowell's father also has a humour: it is anxiety about his son's behaviour. Bobadill, a cowardly soldier, is one of Jonson's best-drawn characters.

[16] *inspired*, showing unusual powers of the mind, as if influenced by some outside spirit; *inspiration*, such an influence.

Jonson wrote about twenty plays alone, and others with other playwrights. His tragedy *Sejanus* was played at the Globe Theatre in 1603 by Shakespeare's company. *Volpone the Fox,* a comedy, was also acted at the Globe, and at the two old universities in 1606.

Jonson was also one of the best producers of masques at this or any other time. These masques are dramatic entertainments with dancing and music, which are more important than the story and the characters.

Jonson was proud and rude. He said, in effect, 'Here is my play. It's good. If you don't like it, that's your fault.' He scorned much of the other dramatic work of the time, but not Shakespeare's. Of him Jonson said:

> Soul of the Age!
> The applause! delight! the wonder of our stage!
> My Shakespeare, rise! I will not lodge[A] thee by
> Chaucer, or Spenser, or bid Beaumont lie
> A little further, to make thee a room.
> Thou art a moniment[B] without a tomb[C],
> And art alive still, while thy book doth live,
> And we have wits[D] to read, and praise to give.
> [A] place (you beside) [B] gravestone [C] grave [D] skill

Jonson believed in the unities of place, time and action. That is to say, he thought that the scenes of a play ought all to be in one place, or at least not too far from each other. If the audience were supposed to travel a few hundred miles between one scene and the next, he did not think it reasonable. The unity of time meant that the events of a play ought not to spread over more than twenty-four hours; and most of his own plays follow this rule. The unity of action meant that nothing outside the main story should be allowed into the play. He crossed out a fine speech in the original *Every Man in his Humour* because it was in praise of poetry and did not suit the rest of the action.

Among his other plays are *Every Man out of his Humour* (1599), *Epicoene, The Silent Woman* (1609), *The Alchemist*[17] (1610) and

[17] *alchemist,* an early scientist.

A dress designed by Inigo Jones for one of the characters in Ben Jonson's masque Chloridia performed in 1631

An illustration from the title page of the play Phylaster written by Beaumont and Fletcher in 1620

Bartholomew Fair (1614). They are all remarkable plays, but it is hard to find a single ordinary person in them.

Other dramatists of the time include JOHN WEBSTER, who depended a lot on violence, revenge, murder, wrong-doing, and so on. His best two plays are *The White Devil* (1611?) and *The Duchess of Malfi* (1614), both of which are frightening. He is not afraid of showing almost unbearable suffering; yet his work contains groups of words that stay long in the mind. Among these are, 'The friendless bodies of unburied men', from *The White Devil*, and 'I am Duchess of Malfi still' and 'I know death hath ten thousand several doors for men to take their exits[18], from *The Duchess of Malfi*.

FRANCIS BEAUMONT and JOHN FLETCHER together wrote a number of plays at this time, and perhaps Fletcher also worked with Shakespeare. With Beaumont he produced *The Knight of the Burning Pestle*[19] (1607), a comedy which helps the modern reader to understand the theatre and stage of those days. The two men also wrote tragedies, such as *The Maid's Tragedy* (1611).

[18] *exit*, a way out.
[19] *pestle*, instrument for beating.

This picture of 1658 shows Oliver Cromwell standing on Error and Fiction. The three figures on the column on the right are **England, Scotland and Ireland**

Chapter Five

John Milton and his time

It is generally agreed that the English poet second after Shakespeare is JOHN MILTON, born in London and educated at Christ's College, Cambridge. After leaving the university, he studied at home in Horton, Buckinghamshire (1632–7), and was grateful to his father for allowing him to do this instead of preparing for a profession. He lived a pure life, believing that he had a great purpose to complete. At college he was known as The Lady of Christ's.

It is convenient to consider his works in three divisions. At first he wrote his shorter poems at Horton. Next he wrote mainly prose. His three greatest poems belong to the last group.

At the age of 23 he had still done little in life, as he admits in a sonnet:

> How soon hath time, the subtle[A] thief of youth
> Stolen on his wing my three-and-twentieth year!
> My hasting days fly on with full career[B]
> And my late spring no bud[C] or blossom[D] showeth.
>
> [A] secretly clever [B] at full speed [C] young flower [D] full flower

Among his other sonnets, he wrote one on his own blindness:

> When I consider how my light is spent
> Ere[A] half my days, in this dark world and wide,
>
> [A] before (I have lived)

And that one talent[B] which is death to hide
Lodged with me useless, though my soul more bent[C]
To serve therewith[D] my Maker, and present
My true account, lest he returning chide[E]
'Doth God exact[F] day-labour, light denied?'
I fondly[G] ask. But Patience, to prevent
That murmur[H], soon replies, 'God doth not need
Either man's work or his own gifts; who best
Bear his mild yoke[I], they serve him best: his state
Is kingly; thousands at his bidding[J] speed[K]
And post[L] o'er land and ocean without rest;
They also serve who only stand and wait.'

[B] ability (to see)   [C] wishing   [D] with it   [E] blame me   [F] demand
[G] foolishly   [H] complaint   [I] service   [J] orders   [K] run   [L] rush

Milton's studies at Horton were deep and wide. One of his notebooks contains pieces taken from eighty writers – Greek, Latin, English, French and Italian. At the same time he was studying music.

L'Allegro (the happy man) and *Il Penseroso* (the thoughtful man) (both 1632) are usually considered together. (The word *Penseroso* should be *Pensieroso* in good Italian.) In the first the poet describes the joys of life in the country in spring; outside in the fields in the morning, but at home in the evening, enjoying music and books. In the second poem, which is set in the autumn, he studies during the day and goes to a great church in the evening to listen to the splendid music.

Comus (1634), also written at Horton, is a masque, and *Arcades* (1633?) part of one. The music for these was written by Henry Lawes, a musician to King Charles I. *Lycidas* (1637) is a sorrowful pastoral on the death by drowning of Edward King, who had been a student with Milton at Cambridge. In one part the poet argues that some men might think it useless to study hard, but the hope of fame drives the spirit onwards:

Were it not better done, as others use,
To sport with Amaryllis in the shade,
Or with the tangles[A] of Neaera's hair?

[A] confusion

Fame is the spur^B that the clear spirit doth raise
(That last infirmity^C of noble mind)
To scorn delights and live laborious^D days.

^B driving force   ^C weakness   ^D hard-working

Milton's prose works were mainly concerned with church affairs, divorce[1], and freedom. Many of them are violent in language, and have neither literary value nor interest for modern readers. The arguments about religion we may neglect entirely. The divorce pamphlets[2] were mainly the result of his own hasty marriage (1643) to Mary Powell, a girl of seventeen. (It was not a success.)

His best prose work is probably the *Areopagitica* (1644), *A Speech for the Liberty of Unlicensed Printing*. This is good writing, and it contains little of the violent language of the other pamphlets. Calm reasoning and smooth words go together, and the style is fairly simple. Milton's sincere belief in the importance of freedom of writing and speech fills the book with honest feeling. Here are three sayings taken from it:

Opinion in good men is but knowledge in the making.

He who destroys a good book kills reason itself.

A good book is the precious life-blood of a master spirit.

The English civil[3] war between Charles I and Parliament (Cromwell) began in 1642 and lasted until 1646; and it was followed by the second civil war, 1648-51. During these years Milton worked hard at his pamphlets, supported Cromwell, and became a minister of the government. His eyesight began to fail, and by 1651 he was totally blind. He became unpopular when Charles II was made king (1660), but it was from this time onwards that he wrote his three greatest works.

He considered several subjects for his great poem, and at one time wanted to write on King Arthur; but he finally chose the fall of the angels, the story of Adam and Eve, and their failure to keep God's

---

[1] *divorce,* ending a marriage while both husband and wife are alive.

[2] *pamphlet,* a composition in a few pages on a particular subject.

[3] *civil* (war), between people of the same nation.

The fallen angels are driven into hell, from Paradise Lost 1688 edition

commands. This great epic poem, *Paradise* [4] *Lost* (first printed in 1667 and sold for £10) was planned in ten books, but written in twelve. The scene is the whole universe, including Heaven and Hell. Milton's splendid voice can be heard here at its best, in the great

[4] *paradise*, Heaven.

blank verse, strengthened by his immense learning and ornamented by all the skill of a master poet. Hell is described like this:

A dungeon^A horrible^B, on all sides round
As one great furnace^C flamed – yet from those flames
No light, but rather darkness visible^D
Served only to discover sights of woe^E
Regions^F of sorrow, doleful^G shades, where peace
And rest can never dwell^H, hope never comes
That comes to all.

^A prison   ^B terrible   ^C fierce fire   ^D which can be seen   ^E sorrow
^F places   ^G sad   ^H live

Paradise Lost contains hundreds of remarkable thoughts put into musical verse. The following are some of these:

The mind is its own place, and in itself
Can make a heaven of hell, a hell of heaven.

(Book 1, 254.)

Better to reign^A in hell than serve in heaven.
^A rule   (Book 1, 263.)

For who would lose
Though full of pain, this intellectual^A being
These thoughts that wander through eternity^B?
^A of the mind   ^B endless time   (Book 2, 146.)

Long is the way
And hard, that out of hell leads up to light.

(Book 2, 432.)

So farewell^A hope, and with hope farewell fear.
^A good-bye   (Book 4, 108.)

Like Marlowe, Milton understood the beauty of proper names. There are many examples of this in *Paradise Lost*. Here are three:

Thick as autumnal leaves that strow^A the brooks^B
In Vallombrosa, where the Etrurian shades
High over-arched embower^C
^A cover   ^B streams   ^C form a roof   (Book 1, 302)

> All who since ...
> Jousted[A] in Aspramont or Montalban,
> Damasco, or Marocco, or Trebisond,
> Or whom Biserta sent from Afric shore
> When Charlemain with all his peerage[B] fell
> By Fontarabbia.
> [A] fought as knights do   [B] nobles   (Book 1, 582)

> As when to them who sail
> Beyond the Cape of Hope and now are past
> Mozambic, off at sea north-east winds blow
> Sabaean odours[A] from the spicy[B] shore
> Of Araby the Blest.
> [A] smells   [B] sweet-smelling   (Book 4, 159)

Paradise Regained (published 1671) is more severe, less splendid than *Paradise Lost*, yet occasionally it also shows the same use of names. These call up rich images for the reader to whom they are familiar, and add to the power and beauty of the sound when the lines are read aloud:

> Of faery damsels[A] met in forest wide
> By knights of Logres[B] or of Lyones[B],
> Lancelot,[C] or Pelleas,[C] or Pellenore.[C]
> [A] spirit-like girls   [B] countries in the stories of King Arthur
> [C] knights of King Arthur's Round Table   Book 1.)

Samson Agonistes (1671), a tragedy on the Greek model, describes the last days of Samson, when he is blind and a prisoner of the Philistines at Gaza. He is forced to go away to provide amusement for the Philistine lords; but later a messenger arrives to say that Samson has pulled down the whole theatre on their heads and his own. Milton had now been blind for about twenty years, and about three years later he died. Samson's sorrows no doubt reminded him of his own, and some of the lines of *Samson* probably reflect Milton's personal feelings:

> A little onward lend thy guiding hand
> To these dark steps, a little further on.

O dark, dark, dark, amid the blaze[A] of noon
Irrecoverably[B] dark, total eclipse[C],
Without all hope of day.

And I shall shortly[D] be with them that rest.
[A] brightness   [B] without cure   [C] darkening   [D] soon

LYRIC POETS. Though Milton towers above all other poets of the time, several lyric-writers have left us sweet songs.

RICHARD LOVELACE wrote *To Althea, from Prison* ('Stone walls do not a prison make, Nor iron bars a cage') and *To Lucasta, on Going to the Wars*, which includes the famous words, 'I could not love thee, Dear, so much, Loved I not honour more'.

SIR JOHN SUCKLING was a famous wit[5] at court. He is a light-hearted and often careless poet:

Out upon it![A] I have loved
    Three whole days together,
And am like to love thee more
    If it prove[B] fair weather.
[A]curse   [B]is

ROBERT HERRICK was considered by the men of his own time to be the best living lyric poet. He writes well about the English country and its flowers. His love songs are also sweet:

I dare not ask a kiss;
I dare not beg a smile;
Lest having that or this,
I might grow proud the while.

No, no, the utmost[A] share
Of my desire shall be
Only to kiss that air
That lately kissed thee.
[A] greatest   (TO ELECTRA)

[5] *wit*, the ability to use language in a clever and amusing way; *a wit*, a person respected for this ability; adj. *witty*.

King Charles I and Queen Henrietta Maria

At about this time EDMUND WALLER wrote some of the earliest heroic couplets, a form of verse which was widely used in the next hundred and fifty years.

In this metre a couplet is a pair of lines, rhyming and of five iambic feet. Waller wrote *His Majesty's Escape* in the metre, probably about 1625. He has been honoured for inventing the heroic couplet but there are other poets for whom the claim is made. They include Shakespeare, who wrote in *Othello,* long before Waller's poem:

> She that was ever fair and never proud;
> Had tongue at will, and yet was never loud;
> Never lacked gold and yet went never gay,
> Fled[A] from her wish, and yet said, 'Now I may.'
> She that, being angered, her revenge being nigh,[B]
> Bade[C] her wrong stay, and her displeasure fly.
>
> [A] ran away   [B] near   [C] ordered   (OTHELLO Act 2, Scene 1.)

Before leaving the poetry of the period[6] we should notice the poem *Cooper's Hill,* written by SIR JOHN DENHAM and published in 1642.

[6] *period,* a certain number of years considered as a unit for the purpose of studying the literature (etc.) of the time.

In between descriptions of the English countryside are Denham's thoughts on various subjects. Four lines on the River Thames are well known:

> O could I flow like thee and make thy stream
> My great example, as it is my theme[A]!
> Though deep, yet clear; though gentle, yet not dull;
> Strong without rage; without o'erflowing full.

[A] subject

A small book in prose, *Microcosmographie* (1628) by JOHN EARLE, offered character studies of ordinary people. It is important because the description of characters of this sort was a basis for character-writing in the novel, not yet born.

SIR THOMAS BROWNE, a doctor, wrote in his difficult, learned and polished style on various subjects. His *Religio Medici* (1642) is a book on religion but includes opinions on many other subjects. *Vulgar Errors*, his longest work, is a study of the mistaken beliefs of the poorly educated, such as the idea that an elephant's legs have no joints.

The period produced a number of very interesting biographies.[7] A good example is the life of his friend John Donne, the poet, written in 1640 by IZAAK WALTON. It was written in excellent prose, but it is also interesting as a source[8] of information on the social history of the time. The work by Izaak Walton that is still widely read and loved is the *Compleat Angler* (1653), a prose discussion of the art of river fishing which includes loving descriptions of riverside scenery and breaks off for verse and songs and then for advice on preparing and cooking the fish:

> This dish of meat[A] is too good for any but anglers,[B] or very honest men.

[A] cooked fish   [B] men who fish with rod and line

The closing of the theatres in 1642 meant that no important drama was produced in the years before 1660.

[7] *biography*, an account of the life of one person.
[8] *source;* a piece of writing which gives information about something.

Part of a scene from The Beggar's Opera *by John Gay painted by William Hogarth*

*Illustrations for
Sheridan's play
'The School for Scandal'
from the first Dublin
edition of 1785 (left)
and for a Comedy
of Manners
'The Careless Husband'
showing the rich
dress of the ladies*

Chapter Six

Restoration drama and prose

When Charles II became king in 1660, the change in English literature was almost as great as the change in government. For one thing, the theatres opened again, and new dramatists therefore appeared.

The tragic drama of this period was made up mainly of heroic plays. In these the men are splendidly brave, and the women wonderfully beautiful. There is a lot of shouting and a good deal of nonsense. The plays are written in heroic couplets, a form of metre perfected by JOHN DRYDEN.

One of Dryden's best heroic plays is *The Conquest of Granada* (1670). In addition to the usual loud language, the play contains some good lyrics. There are other good things in it:

> I am as free as nature first made man,
> Ere[A] the base laws of servitude[B] began,
> When wild in woods the noble savage[C] ran.
>
> [A] before   [B] slavery   [C] wild man

Another of his better heroic plays is *Aurengzebe* (1676), which is based on a struggle for empire in India. It is his last rhymed play and contains one of the finest speeches that Dryden ever wrote:

> When I consider life, 'tis all a cheat;
> Yet fooled with hope, men favour the deceit;

* *restoration*, the period after the restoration, or return to rule by kings, in 1660 after twenty years of rule by Parliament.

Trust on, and think tomorrow will repay.
Tomorrow's falser than the former day;
Lies worse, and while it says we shall be blest
With some new joys, cuts off what we possessed.   (IV.i.)

In most of Dryden's plays, fine speeches and poor ones may follow
each other in an astonishing way. He seems to have been unable to
see his own faults. His first comedy, *Marriage-à-la-Mode*, in bad blank
verse, appeared in 1672. Its subject is explained in the first song:

Why should a foolish marriage vow[A]
   Which long ago was made,
Oblige[B] us to each other now
   When passion[C] is decayed?

[A] promise   [B] force us to stay with   [C] strong feeling (love)

His well-known play, *All for Love* (or *The World Well Lost*) (1678)
is in blank verse. It is based on Shakespeare's *Antony and Cleopatra*.
We may well be surprised that he tried to improve on Shakespeare,
but we have to remember that in his day *Antony and Cleopatra*
was not valued very highly. He said that *All for Love* was the only
play that he wrote to please himself. Some critics consider it his
best, but others prefer *Don Sebastian* (1691). This was based on
the possibility that Sebastian, King of Portugal, had not, after all,
been killed in battle.

Few or none of Dryden's plays are acted now. They are strangely
unequal; there is usually some good, and some bad, writing in
each. The poetry of the rhymed plays is on the whole better, and
the dramatic force of the unrhymed plays is stronger.

Some of the men of the time saw the stupidity of the extra-
ordinary situations in the heroic plays, and the second Duke of
Buckingham, probably with some help, produced a comedy,
The Rehearsal[2] (1672), which satirized[3] them. The plot is intentionally foolish, and hits at Dryden and other dramatists.

[2] *rehearsal*, practising a play before it is acted in public.
[3] *satire*, a composition intended to show the foolishness of some person or
custom and invite the laughter of the reader or hearer; the writer, or
satirist, usually pretends to accept as sensible the thing he really wants to
satirize; adj. *satirical*.

Of the tragedies by other dramatists, three by THOMAS OTWAY are among the best. These are *Don Carlos* (1676) in rhymed verse; *The Orphan*[4] (1680) in blank verse; and *Venice Preserved* (1682) also in blank verse. He also wrote other plays, and used the works of the French dramatists Racine and Molière as a basis for two. Otway died very poor at the early age of 33.

Venice Preserved, his best play, was well received. In this, Jaffier, a young nobleman of Venice, marries Belvidera, the daughter of the noble Priuli. He then asks Priuli for money, but is insulted. He joins a plot against the State of Venice, but his wife, anxious in mind, persuades him to tell Priuli about it. Nothing can then save the conspirators. Belvidera goes mad and dies, and Jaffier kills himself.

A new kind of comedy appeared at the end of this century, known as the Comedy of Manners. This kind of play is hard and bright, witty and heartless. It was introduced by SIR GEORGE ETHEREGE His play *The Man of Mode* (1676) gives a picture of the immoral manners of the society of the day, but has no proper plot. WILLIAM WYCHERLEY was a satirical dramatist. His best works are *The Country Wife* (1675), a coarse play with some fine wit in it; and *The Plain Dealer* (1676), which was perhaps modelled on Molière's *Le Misanthrope* and is his best play.

Better than these were the plays of WILLIAM CONGREVE. At the end of the century, when he was writing, the coarseness of the early days of the Restoration was beginning to pass away, and the more reasonable eighteenth century was near. His first comedy, *The Old Bachelor*[5] (1693), is about an old fellow who pretends to hate women, but marries a bad one. An amusing character in this play is a foolish knight, Sir Joseph Wittol. *The Double Dealer* (1694) is concerned with angry lovers. *Love for Love* (1695) is funnier, and contains clever speeches and interesting, but foolish, characters.

These three comedies follow the pattern of Etherege's polished style; but *The Way of the World* (1700) is finer than any other play of the time. The drawing of the characters especially of the women, is good, and so is the prose. Unfortunately it was not well received, and Congreve stopped writing plays in disgust.

4 *orphan*, child whose parents are dead.
5 *bachelor*, unmarried man.

SIR JOHN VANBRUGH wrote three successful comedies, *The Relapse* (1696), *The Provoked Wife* (1697) and *The Confederacy* (1705). His characters are distinct, his plots interesting, but his writing unremarkable. He was an architect[6] by profession, and was responsible for the building of several important houses. When he was buried, his epitaph[7] was:

> Lie heavy on him, Earth, for he
> Laid many a heavy load on thee.

These plays were in general rather coarse, clever, bright, and partly a reflection of the behaviour of upper-class society of the time. But not all people of the day were like the characters in them. Many were reading Milton's *Paradise Lost*, and nothing could be more different from a Restoration comedy. Others read the *Pilgrim's Progress* (1678), John Bunyan's great allegory of Christian's journey to heaven through the evils of the world.

Much later, in 1773, OLIVER GOLDSMITH produced *She Stoops*[8] *to Conquer*, a play in which a private house is mistaken for a hotel. (Such an event actually happened.) RICHARD BRINSLEY SHERIDAN wrote *The Rivals* (1775) at about that time. In this play Mrs Malaprop mixes up long words and therefore talks a lot of funny nonsense. Sheridan's *The School for Scandal*[9] (1777) introduces three characters whose love of scandal is so great that they "strike a character [i.e. reputation] dead at every word'. This cheerful comedy also contains a well-known drinking song. Here is a verse of it:

> Here's to[A] the charmer whose dimples[B] we prize
>   Here's to the maid[C] who has none, sir.
> Here's to the girl with a pair of blue eyes
>   And here's to the nymph[D] with but one, sir.

[A] good health to   [B] small hollows in the skin (a sign of beauty)   [C] girl
[D] girl (woodland spirit)

[6] *architect*, a man who prepares the plans for buildings.
[7] *epitaph*, words written for (cutting on) a gravestone.
[8] *stoop*, make oneself humble.
[9] *scandal*, talk in which the reputation of other people is attacked.

Sheridan's third important play is *The Critic* (1779). It is a satire rather like Buckingham's *The Rehearsal*, and it satirizes drama and literary criticism. There is a foolish play in it, written by one of the characters; when this is acted, its author discusses its qualities with two critics. The result is very funny.

We must now consider the prose of the Restoration time. Dryden's critical works include his *Essay on Dramatic Poesie* (1668). This compared English and French drama, defended the use of rhyme in drama, and praised Shakespeare. Dryden's prose is important. More than anyone else at this time he led the way to a clear, reasonable and balanced way of writing English. In addition to this he was a better critic than most poets. In the *Essay* he mentioned the limitations which the French set themselves by keeping to the unities of time and place.

JOHN BUNYAN's prose set an example of clear, simple expression, especially in *The Pilgrim's Progress* and *The Holy War* (1682), another allegory, in which he was helped by his own experiences as a soldier on the side of Parliament in the civil war. His style was influenced by his regular reading of the Authorised Version of the Bible and it reflects the beauty and earnest simplicity of that translation. *The Pilgrim's Progress* has given the English language some names of places (for example, Vanity Fair,[10] Doubting Castle, the Slough of Despond[11]) and people (for example, the Giant[12] Despair and Mr Greatheart) which are household words.

JOHN LOCKE's prose was also clear, earnest and without ornament, though it lacks the balance in its sentences which gives Bunyan's style its charm. But Locke's *Essay on the Human Understanding* (1690) is one of the most important works of English philosophy. It gave a new direction to thought, not only in England but in other countries of Europe although, as Locke himself warned:

> New opinions are always suspected, and usually opposed, without any other reason but because they are not already common.

[10] *Vanity Fair*, the world – seen as a market-place *(fair)* of empty foolishness.
[11] *the Slough of Despond*, a time of great discouragement – seen as a dangerous place of watery ground *(slough)*.
[12] *giant*, a man of more than human size.

The first picture in John Bunyan's The Pilgrim's Progress
which he began to write in 1675

A part of Samuel Pepys' Diary, which he kept from 1660-69, and an explanation of the same passage

SAMUEL PEPYS wrote a well-known diary[13] which opens on January 1st, 1660, and ends on May 31st, 1669, when his eyesight began to fail. The diary was written in secret signs, and remained unread at a Cambridge college until 1825, when it was successfully read. It is interesting and important; it gives details of many events and of the life of that time. The character of Pepys himself, as shown by his diary, is very attractive.

Another diarist, JOHN EVELYN, describes his travels in Europe, and writes about the men of his own time. The diary was first published in 1818. Evelyn also wrote several books on art and trees.

[13] *diary*, daily record of events.

"*The Morning Walk*" *by Thomas Gainsborough, who lived from 1727 to 1788. The painting illustrates the dress and customs of the age*

Chapter Seven

English poets, 1660–1798

Most of DRYDEN's poetry -- chiefly satire and translations – is written in his excellent rhymed couplets. Yet an early poem, *Annus Mirabilis* (1667), is in four-line stanzas. It describes the chief events of 'The Wonderful Year', 1666. These events are the war against Holland and The Great Fire of London. The work is unequal. The first part (about the war) is not as good as the second (about the fire).

Dryden's great satire, *Absalom and Achitophel* (1681) uses a Bible story as a basis on which to attack politicians. Another of Dryden's satires, *MacFlecknoe*, (1682) attacks a rival poet, Shadwell. A bad poet whose name was Flecknoe had recently died; and in this poem Dryden treats his own enemy Shadwell as Flecknoe's son. Flecknoe is made to say:

> Shadwell alone my perfect image bears[A]
> Mature[B] in dullness from his tender years.
> Shadwell alone of all my sons is he
> Who stands confirmed[C] in full stupidity.
> The rest to some faint meaning make pretence,
> But Shadwell never deviates[D] into sense.
>
> [A] is exactly like me   [B] developed   [C] fixed; rooted   [D] changes direction

Dryden's splendid command of the heroic couplet helped him to write biting satires. This kind of scorn, together with the polished and forceful verse, has seldom been bettered by others.

Among Dryden's best short poems are two songs, not in heroic metre: The *Ode for Saint Cecilia's Day* (1687) and *Alexander's Feast* (1697).

Dryden's translations, which he wrote in the later years of his life, included the (Latin) satires of Juvenal, the whole of Virgil (which brought him £1,200) and parts of Horace and Ovid. From the Greek he also translated parts of Homer and Theocritus.

ALEXANDER POPE, a follower of Dryden in verse but not in drama, used the couplet as a smooth but steely tool. His health was bad, and he thought of life as a long illness. While still young, he wrote his *Essay on Criticism* (1711). Like much of his work, it contains sayings often remembered today:

> A little learning is a dangerous thing.

> True wit is nature to advantage dressed,
> What oft was thought but ne'er so well expressed.

> True ease in writing comes from art, not chance,
> As those move easiest who have learned to dance.

> Where'er you find 'the cooling western breeze[A]'
> In the next line it 'whispers through the trees'.
> If crystal[B] streams 'with pleasing murmurs[C] creep'
> The reader's threatened, not in vain, with 'sleep'.
> Then at the last and only couplet fraught[D]
> With some unmeaning thing they call a thought,
> A needless Alexandrine[E] ends the song
> That, like a wounded snake, drags its slow length along.

[A] gentle wind   [B] clear   [C] soft sounds   [D] loaded   [E] an Alexandrine is a line like the last with 6 instead of 5 feet

Pope's delightful poem *The Rape of the Lock* [= The stealing of the hair] (1712-4) takes a light subject and treats it as important. Lord Petre had cut off some hair from Miss Arabella Fermor's head and the two families had quarrelled violently. Pope tried to end the quarrel by writing this 'heroic' poem, describing the event in detail; but he only made the quarrel worse.

Pope also translated the *Iliad* and the *Odyssey* of Homer. His *Imitations of Horace* (1733-9), in the heroic couplet, are sometimes very bitter. In his satire *The Dunciad* (1728), an attack on dullness, he laughs at poor poets who are writing for their bread – a cruel thing to do. The work gives little pleasure now. His later poem, the *Essay on Man* (1732-4), shows that he knew little philosophy, but the verse has the usual polish. He wrote four *Moral Essays* (1731-5), the first about the characters of men and the second about the characters of women ('Most women have no characters at all'). The last two essays deal with the proper use of riches.

The same heroic metre was used by OLIVER GOLDSMITH in two poems which are, and deserve to be, popular. These are *The Traveller* (1764) and *The Deserted Village* (1770). The 'village' is an Irish one, whose people have been driven away by bigger landowners. The poem charmingly describes a life which has now gone for ever:

> There in his noisy mansion[A], skilled to rule,
> The village master kept his little school.
> A man severe he was, and stern[B] to view;
> I knew him well, and every truant[C] knew.
> Well had the boding[D] tremblers learned to trace[E]
> The day's disasters[F] in his morning face.
> Full well they laughed with counterfeited[G] glee [H]
> At all his jokes, for many a joke had he.
>
> [A] big house   [B] severe   [C] runaway   [D] anxious   [E] see   [F] terrible events
> [G] false   [H] laughter

The eighteenth century is often called The Age of Reason. Order was important in men's thoughts, and the comfortable town was usually preferred to the wild mountains. The heroic couplet is well suited to verse based on reasoning, but it must not be thought that there was no other sort of poetry. A return to thoughts about nature and more lyrical subjects began early.

Pope said that 'The proper study of mankind is man', but JAMES THOMSON chose as his special study *The Seasons*, on which he wrote four poems in blank verse: *Winter* (1726), *Summer* (1727), *Spring* (1728) and *Autumn* (1730). These poems, which were very popular, drew pictures of woods, fields, birds, deserts, and so on. Yet Thomson was unable to escape altogether from the poetic

*An illustration from
James Thomson's poem
The Seasons
showing Summer*

*Below: an old illustration for the opening verse of Thomas Gray's Elegy Written
in a Country Churchyard*

language of the eighteenth century, which meant using unnatural and fixed phrases instead of the usual and natural word. Thomson's other good poem was *The Castle of Indolence* [1] (1748), written in the Spenserian stanza. It is perhaps better poetry than that in *The Seasons*. It is a poet's dream, and the sleepy language has a special beauty.

A group of poets who turned away from the bright tea-table chose death for their subject. They are sometimes known as the churchyard school of poets. EDWARD YOUNG was one of them. His *Night Thoughts*, written in good blank verse, was at one time very popular. Its subjects are life, death, the future world, and God. It is unequal, dark, sad, and filled with strange imaginations. He calls man:

> A worm. A god. I tremble at myself
> And in myself am lost.

In the ninth book he says,

> From human mould[A] we reap[B] our daily bread ...
> Whole buried towns support the dancer's heel[C].

[A] decay   [B] cut corn   [C] back of foot

ROBERT BLAIR was another of this school, and he also used blank verse. In his poem *The Grave* (1743) he begs the dead to come back and tell us something about the grave:

> Tell us, ye dead! Will none of you in pity
> To those you left behind disclose[A] the secret?
> Oh that some courteous[B] ghost would blab[C] it out
> What 'tis you are and we must shortly[D] be!

[A] tell   [B] polite   [C] tell   [D] soon

THOMAS GRAY was a greater poet than these. His *Elegy* [2] *Written in a Country Churchyard* (1750), one of the most beautiful and famous of English poems, describes his thoughts as he looks at the graves of

[1] *indolence*, laziness.
[2] *elegy*, a sad poem for the death of a particular person or the loss of some loved place or thing.

country people buried near the church at Stoke Poges. He wonders what they might have done in the world if they had had better opportunities; but they did not go out into the great cities:

> Far from the madding crowd's ignoble[A] strife[B]
> Their sober[C] wishes never learned to stray[D];
> Along the cool sequestered[E] vale[F] of life
> They kept the noiseless tenor[G] of their way.
>
> [A] not noble   [B] struggle   [C] calm   [D] wander   [E] sheltered   [F] valley   [G] course

Or again:

> Full many a gem[A] of purest ray serene[B]
> The dark unfathomed[C] caves of ocean bear;
> Full many a flower is born to blush[D] unseen
> And waste its sweetness on the desert air.
>
> [A] precious stone   [B] calm   [C] unexplored   [D] redden

Gray's ode,[3] *The Bard*[4] (1757), is intended as a sad song by a Welsh poet, addressed to King Edward I, who put all the Welsh poets to death. He curses Edward and all his race. The ode shows that Gray, like Marlowe and Milton, could use proper names with skill; combined with vowel-music this skill can produce lines like these:

> Cold is Cadwallo's tongue
> That hushed[A] the stormy main[B]
>   Brave Urien sleeps upon his craggy[C] bed.
> Mountains, ye mourn[D] in vain
> Modred, whose magic song
>   Made huge[E] Plynlimmon bow his cloud-topped head.
>
> [A] made quiet   [B] sea   [C] rocky   [D] be sad at a time of death   [E] immense

We may not like the idea that Cadwallo's tongue is 'cold' but there is no doubt that Gray could write great poetry. Notice, too, his use of alliteration.

---

[3] *ode*, a lyric poem addressed to a person or an idea; Gray's *The Bard* is a Pindaric ode, following an exact pattern of stanzas and rhymes, but this classical form is seldom used in English odes.

[4] *bard*, poet.

As a schoolboy Gray went to Eton. In his *Ode on a Distant Prospect of Eton College* (1742) he thinks of the boys still at school and of their present happiness and the troubles that are waiting for them in life:

> Still as they run they look behind;
> They hear a voice in every wind,
>   And snatch[A] a fearful joy.

> Alas![B] Regardless[C] of their doom[D]
> The little victims[E] play!
> No sense have they of ills to come,
> No care beyond today.

[A] catch   [B] Oh!   [C] not caring about   [D] fate   [E] persons who will be sacrificed

Gray's other poems include an *Ode on a Favourite Cat* (1747), which was drowned. In later life he learnt Icelandic and wrote poems on Icelandic and Celtic subjects. He is also famous for some fine letters.

Other poets turned to the past when they tried to escape from the polished orderliness of the eighteenth century. Thomas Percy's *Reliques*[5] *of Ancient English Poetry* (1765) brought to light many old poems from the darkness of the past. A stranger book was *Fragments*[6] *of Ancient Poetry* (1760) by JAMES MACPHERSON. He pretended that he had found some old poems by a poet, Ossian; but he wrote most of them himself. In much the same way THOMAS CHATTERTON invented a fifteenth-century poet, Thomas Rowley, whose poems he pretended to have. The trick was discovered, but the poems are good in spite of that – better, in fact, than some poems that Chatterton wrote under his own name.

WILLIAM BLAKE, a poet and an artist, illustrated[7] the works of Young, Blair, Gray and others. Much of his poetry has hidden meanings that are hard to understand. He did not believe in the reality of matter, or in the power of earthly rulers, or in punishment

[5] *reliques*, remains.
[6] *fragments*, bits.
[7] *illustrate*, to make pictures of scenes, characters or actions described in a book; the *illustrations* may explain, add interest to, or just ornament the printed words.

The Blossom.

Merry Merry Sparrow
Under leaves so green
A happy Blossom
Sees you swift as arrow
Seek your cradle narrow
Near my Bosom.

Pretty Pretty Robin
Under leaves so green
A happy Blossom
Hears you sobbing sobbing
Pretty Pretty Robin
Near my Bosom.

A page illustrated by Blake from the original version of his poems
The Songs of Innocence and Experience

after death. His best known works include *Songs of Innocence* (1787) and *Songs of Experience* (1794). The second is darker and heavier than the first; but it does contain some good poems. Here is a verse from *The Tiger*:

> Tiger, tiger, burning bright
> In the forests of the night,
> What immortal[A] hand or eye
> Could frame thy fearful symmetry[B]?
>
> [A] undying   [B] perfect shape

ROBERT BURNS was a Scottish farmer whose lyrics became famous. (The second edition of his poems brought him £500.) He wrote hundreds of songs and lyrics, and among them *Mary Morrison, John Anderson* and *The Banks of Doon* are famous. His love-songs include 'My love's like a red, red rose'. He had a deep understanding of animals and love for them. Even a mouse brought a gentle poem from his pen.

One more eighteenth-century poet is worth our special notice: WILLIAM COWPER's verse shows the beginning of the swing away from the formal classical style of Pope towards the simpler, more natural expression which we shall see in Wordsworth and Coleridge (p. 91). These lines are from Cowper's long poem, *The Task*[8] (1784):

> Now stir the fire, and close the shutters[A] fast,
> Let fall the curtains, wheel the sofa[B] round,
> And, while the bubbling[C] and loud-hissing[D] urn[E]
> Throws up a steamy column,[F] and the cups,
> That cheer but not inebriate,[G] wait on each,
> So let us welcome peaceful evening in.
>
> [A] window covers   [B] comfortable seat   [C] boiling   [D] making a boiling sound
> [E] large tea vessel   [F] narrow cloud of steam   [G] act like strong drink

[8] *task*, a piece of work to be done.

A coffee house in the early eighteenth century. At this time coffee houses were social centres for discussion of news, politics and the arts

Chapter Eight

Eighteenth-century prose

The new century threw aside the strange plots and ideas of heroic tragedy and turned to reasonable things. DANIEL DEFOE described the Great Plague[1] of London in his *Journal of the Plague Year* (1722). The plague broke out (badly) in 1665, when Defoe was only five, but he obtained information about it from different places. His *Robinson Crusoe* (1719) is a better and more famous book. This story is based on a real event. Alexander Selkirk, a sailor who quarrelled with his captain, was in fact put on the island of Juan Fernandez, near Chile, and lived there alone for four years. Defoe made a good story out of this event: indeed, his book is almost a novel, and one of the first in English.

RICHARD STEELE and JOSEPH ADDISON worked together in producing *The Tatler*, a paper of essays on various subjects. A more famous paper, *The Spectator*, followed. Steele was a warm-hearted man, friendly and careless with money. Addison was a calm man of learning, and a traveller, and he hated violence. These essays, written in pure English prose without too much ornament, helped towards the production of the novel; for they described the actions of imaginary characters, such as Sir Roger de Coverley, who became a great favourite among the readers.

Addison and Steele were mild; JONATHAN SWIFT was a bitter satirist. At this time there was a fierce argument about the abilities and the books of the ancients and the moderns. In this battle of

---

[1] *plague*, a dangerous disease.

Robinson Crusoe's Island from the 1720 edition of the book

the books Swift supported his friend Temple by writing *The Battle of the Books* (1704) on the side of the ancients. His *Tale of a Tub* (1704) attacked religious ideas, and annoyed a large number of readers. An example of his bitterness may be seen in *A Modest Proposal* (1729), which contains the suggestion that the poor, who needed money, should sell their children to the rich as food. This kind of satire seriously accepts the evils of the world, and goes on to show their extreme results.

Swift's most famous satire, *Gulliver's Travels* (1726), is in four books. As a story it is popular with the young, who usually read the first two books: Gulliver's voyages to Lilliput (where the people are six inches high) and Brobdingnag (where they are immense). The Lilliputians fight wars (as the English do) which seem foolish. The king of Brobdingnag, after hearing about Gulliver's country, thinks that the people there must be the most hateful race of creatures on earth.

DR SAMUEL JOHNSON was always poor and therefore had to do all kinds of literary work, even if he did not like it. His famous *Dictionary* appeared in 1755 and went into five editions[2] in his own life. He was a kind of literary ruler, giving judgments on books and authors like a god. Late in life he wrote his *Lives of the Poets* (1779-81) with decision and clear expression.

His own writings are less important than what he said, and a record of his conversations has fortunately been preserved for us in the *Life of Johnson* (1791) by his friend JAMES BOSWELL. This is the

[2] *edition*, printing of a book with (in 2nd and later *editions*) corrections and other changes.

greatest biography in English. Boswell had the happy idea of writing down the exact words used by Johnson, and the result is a highly interesting picture of the literary world of the time. Here are a few of Johnson's statements:

A man, Sir, should keep his friendship in constant[A] repair.

Let me smile with the wise and feed with the rich.

It matters not how a man dies, but how he lives.

Why, Sir, if you were to read Richardson for the story, your impatience would be so much fretted[B] that you would hang yourself.

Sir, there is more knowledge of the heart in one letter of Richardson's than in all *Tom Jones*.

There is now less flogging[C] in our great schools than formerly, but then less is learned there; so that what the boys get at one end they lose at the other.

Sir, when a man is tired of London, he is tired of life; for there is in London all that life can afford[D].

[A] continual   [B] worried   [C] beating   [D] give

An original picture of Dr Johnson and Boswell on a journey to Scotland

Johnson's *Rasselas, Prince of Abyssinia* (1759) is a kind of novel; at least it has a story. But there are many essays on various subjects. Rasselas, his sister Nekayah, and the philosopher Imlac go to Egypt to study, because Rasselas is tired of the easy life in Abyssinia. Johnson wrote the book in one week to pay for his mother's funeral.

EDWARD GIBBON decided to write *The Decline and Fall of the Roman Empire* while he was making a tour of Italy in 1764. The first book appeared in 1776, two more books in 1781, and the last three in 1788. This is recognised as the greatest historical work in English literature. In splendid prose it covers the events of thirteen centuries, and relates the ancient to the modern world. It is clear and complete, and usually correct. It deals with various religions, Roman law, Persian politics, the attacks of uncivilised tribes, and many other affairs. After more than twenty years of search and study, Gibbon says, 'it was on the day, or rather the night, of the 27th of June, 1787, between the hours of eleven and twelve that I wrote the last line of the last page in a summer-house in my garden.'

EDMUND BURKE wrote fine prose too, but it was oratorical[3] prose. He was a lawyer and a member of Parliament. Some of his wise and splendid speeches may be found in his *Speech on American Taxation* (1774), *Speech on Conciliation[4] with America* (1775), and *Letter to the Sheriffs of Bristol* (1777). He argues that wise government must not press its rights too hard. 'The question with me,' he says, 'is not whether you have a right to render [=make] your people miserable, but whether it is not your interest to make them happy.'

Later in his life his *Reflections on the French Revolution[5]* (1790) made him famous in all parts of Europe. He supported the old ways of government against the new. Although this book deals with the problem of that age, its pages are covered with ideas which are true in other situations.

Burke made many other speeches. He wanted to get rid of slavery. He attacked Warren Hastings after Hastings had left India in 1785. He often spoke on parliamentary affairs.

Some of the best English letters were written during the eighteenth century. The post at that time was slow and uncertain, and when

---

[3] *oratory*, making public speeches; *oratorical*, of this style.
[4] *conciliation*, gaining (someone) as a friend.
[5] *revolution*, a rising of the people against their rulers.

anyone wrote a letter it was an important event. LADY MARY WORTLEY MONTAGU wrote some of the best-known. She was a witty, learned and beautiful woman. Her letters from Turkey, where her husband represented the King (George I) of England, describe events in that country, and there she discovered a way of preventing smallpox[6]. She tried it on her own son and introduced it into England. Later she wrote letters from Italy, and all show her wisdom and good sense.

The fourth EARL OF CHESTERFIELD is chiefly famous now for his letters to his son. They are in fine prose, contain wise advice, but are not always morally perfect. He tried to tell his son what would succeed in the world, and not what ought to succeed. Chesterfield also received a famous letter from Dr Johnson, who once asked him for help with his dictionary. Just as the work was finished, Chesterfield praised it in public. Johnson wrote an angry letter asking why a great man should help him when no more help was needed.

The letters of HORACE WALPOLE are written in good prose, but the character of the writer is not always attractive. The letters of the poets Gray and Cowper are also important. Gray's are those of a learned man; Cowper's show us something of his simple and gentle character.

The English novel proper was born about the middle of the eighteenth century. The study of character had begun some time before in Earle's *Microcosmographie* and other books of this kind. Addison and Steele had drawn the character of Sir Roger de Coverley, and had studied the behaviour of women, in *The Spectator*. Dryden and Chesterfield had built up a fine prose style which was ready for use. Defoe in *Robinson Crusoe*, and other writers such as Swift, had written stories of adventure. It is not, therefore, surprising that in 1740 a real novel appeared. It was *Pamela* by SAMUEL RICHARDSON.

Pamela is a novel written in the form of letters, and these appeared one after the other. This book is different from mere stories of adventure; for it examines the human heart and shows the effects of human character. Richardson, a printer by trade, did not write it until he was over fifty. When he did write it, and when the letters began to appear, the ladies of the time were excited. They no

[6] *smallpox*, a dangerous disease which, if it does not kill, leaves deep marks on the skin.

longer needed the old stories of far-away princesses; they could read about the feelings of an English girl, Pamela Andrews. It is a simple story of a good girl who receives the rewards of virtue. Because it came out in letters (supposed to be from Pamela), the ladies could try to persuade Richardson to let Pamela do what they wanted. 'Oh, Mr Richardson, please don't let her die!' and so on.

Richardson's next novel, *Clarissa Harlowe* (1747-8), is his best. Clarissa is the beautiful daughter of a severe father who wants her to marry against her will. She is driven to a state of despair, and dies an early death. The novel is about eight times as long as an ordinary modern novel, but it was widely read in England and abroad in Richardson's day.

HENRY FIELDING, a man of gay character, began a novel, *Joseph Andrews* (1742), as a kind of satire on *Pamela*. Joseph is supposed to be her brother. Pamela was a serving-girl whose master paid her too much attention; Joseph is also a servant and is in difficulties of the same sort. Fielding soon became interested in his own novel, and let Joseph fall into the background. The later part of the novel is chiefly about Parson Adams, a simple, funny, and good-hearted priest. Fielding wrote the novel directly, as a straight story, without the trick of letters.

Fielding's greatest novel, *Tom Jones* (1749), appeared in eighteen books, each of which had an essay before it. (George Eliot and Thackeray did the same sort of thing.) Tom is a boy found in Mr

An illustration by Thomas Rowlandson for Fielding's Tom Jones

Allworthy's house, and he is brought up there with kindness. Then he falls in love with the beautiful Sophia, daughter of Squire Western. He does several other things that Allworthy does not like, and Tom is driven out of the house. In London he has many adventures, but in the end he meets Sophia there and all ends happily.

Another of Fielding's books, *The History of Jonathan Wild the Great* (1743), is a satire. It deals with a real criminal, Wild, who stole a lot of money with his followers before he was found guilty and put to death in 1725.

A new kind of picture of real life was drawn by TOBIAS SMOLLETT in his picaresque novel, *Roderick Random* (1748). The novel is powerful and unpleasant. It describes bitterly the life of those who sail the seas. In another novel, *Peregrine Pickle* (1751), the hero is an unpleasant fellow who travels a good deal, has fights, and visits Paris and Holland. Several well-drawn characters include a violent seaman, Trunnion, whose language is terrible, but whose heart is of gold.

A later novel by Smollett, *Humphrey Clinker* (1771), is in the form of letters, and is less violent and in better taste than the other two. It describes the travels through England and Scotland of the Bramble family. Smollett's books often give us interesting information about life and society in his time.

A fourth novel-writer of importance at this time was LAURENCE STERNE. His astonishing books are as confusing as life itself. He seems to dislike order and common sense, but perhaps life does not contain much of either. His *Tristram Shandy* (1760-7) made him famous. We have to read about half the book before the hero, Tristram, is born. Sterne leaves the story whenever he likes, to give opinions and write essays on any subject in the world. He adds a few blank pages and rows of stars here and there to confuse his readers as much as possible. In spite of this, he can draw clear characters, such as the old soldier, Uncle Toby, and his servant, Trim. Another work by Sterne, *A Sentimental [7] Journey through France and Italy* (1768) is not so confused or confusing and is in better prose. Yet even here Sterne's strange mind looks out at us from the pages.

---

[7] *sentimental*, concerned with the feelings (rather than reason), especially feelings of love.

An illustration from
William Beckford's
"novel of terror" Vathek

Another important novel of the time was *The Vicar of Wakefield* (1761-2) by OLIVER GOLDSMITH. It is the story of a good and virtuous family which has great misfortunes; but all comes right in the end. The novel contains some famous short poems, including the *Elegy on the Death of a Mad Dog*, which shows something of Goldsmith's humour. A good man is bitten by a mad dog:

> The wound it seemed both sore and sad
>   To every Christian eye;
> And while they swore the dog was mad,
>   They swore the man would die.
>
> But soon a wonder came to light
>   That showed the rogues[A] they lied.
> The man recovered[B] of the bite;
>   The dog it was that died.

[A] bad men   [B] got better

HORACE WALPOLE, whose letters have been mentioned, wrote (partly as a joke) *The Castle of Otranto* (1764), a novel about the twelfth and thirteenth centuries. It contains descriptions of impossible events, such as the destruction of a building by an immense ghost inside it. This 'novel of terror'[8] was followed by others. *Vathek* (1786) is a novel by WILLIAM BECKFORD. This astonishing book (first written in French and then translated) tells us that Vathek was the grandson of Harun al-Rashid and became the servant of Eblis, the devil. After many adventures, he is allowed to visit the underground halls of Eblis, but discovers that all the riches and wonders there have little interest for him. He is punished for his crimes with terrible pain. The description of the underworld is a good piece of writing.

MRS ANN RADCLIFFE developed the novel of terror with work of better quality. She had a real feeling for nature. She causes interest by describing unusual scenes and sights, such as moving walls and secret passages, and strange events which she explains later. Her greatest novel, *The Mysteries of Udolpho* (1794), is set in the Appenine Mountains. The girl Emily is held in a castle by her aunt's husband, an evil character. The writer keeps up the reader's interest by describing one astonishing event after another. In a locked room Emily sees a dark curtain and wants to look behind it. She is afraid of what may be there, but she bravely pulls it aside. On a long seat she sees a dead body, with blood on the floor below. She bends over it, faints, and drops her lamp. Mrs Radcliffe mixes this kind of writing with fine descriptions of sunlight on the forests, mountains dark in the evening time (the Alps attracted her greatly), and the sweetness of wild flowers. From her descriptions, it is clear that she looked directly at nature, and did not get her ideas from books. Her other novels were *Romance*[9] *of the Forest* (1791) and *The Italian* (1797). She also wrote *A Sicilian Romance* (1790) and *An Italian Romance* (1791).

[8] *terror*, very great fear.

[9] *romance*, a love story; *romantic*, as or like a love story, not like everyday life but concerned with a world in which love, beauty, and adventure are the most important things.

*A drawing of Tintern Abbey, by Joseph Turner. After a visit to Tintern
Abbey William Wordsworth wrote one of his best known poems*

Chapter Nine

Early nineteenth-century poets

The main stream of poetry in the eighteenth century had been orderly and polished, without much feeling for nature. Heroic couplets were used for this verse, but various writers had broken away from the form and the thought. In spite of this, the publication of the first edition of the *Lyrical Ballads*[1] (1798) came as a shock. The critics considered the language too simple and the change too violent. This important book – the signal of the beginning of the romantic age – was the joint work of WILLIAM WORDSWORTH and SAMUEL TAYLOR COLERIDGE, often known, with Southey, as the Lake Poets, because they liked the lake district in the north-west of England and lived in it.

Wordsworth was a poet of nature, and had the special ability to throw a charm over ordinary things. Coleridge, on the other hand, could make mysterious events acceptable to a reader's mind. Neither of them used the old language of poetry much.

Wordsworth was so filled with the love of nature that, in later editions of the *Lyrical Ballads* (1800-2), he said that the language of poetry ought to be the same as the language of a simple farm-worker. Yet he could not keep to this idea himself; his imagination led him far beyond the life and thoughts of a countryman.

Coleridge's poem, *The Rime of the Ancient Mariner*[2], appeared in the first edition of the *Lyrical Ballads*. An old sailor describes some strange misfortunes that happened to his ship. It was in the ice of the

[1] *ballad*, a simple poem in short stanzas telling a story.
[2] *mariner*, a sailor.

South Pole when he shot a great bird; for this crime a curse fell on the ship. The wind failed, the water-supply ended, and all the other sailors died of thirst. The old mariner was then left:

> Alone, alone, all all alone,
>   Alone on a wide, wide sea,
> And never a saint[A] took pity on
>   My soul in agony[B].
>
> The many men so beautiful!
>   And they all dead did lie.
> And a thousand thousand slimy[C] things
>   Lived on, and so did I.
>
> [A] Holy spirit   [B] great pain   [C] oily

The mysterious surroundings of the silent ship are described in Coleridge's magic words. At last the mariner, seeing God's creatures in the moonlight, blesses them. This breaks the curse and he is able to return home.

Two other important poems by Coleridge (not in the *Lyrical Ballads*) are *Christabel* (1816) and *Kubla Khan* (1816). Neither was finished, but there is again magic in each. Christabel finds the beautiful lady Geraldine in a wood and brings her home. Geraldine claims to be the daughter of an old friend of Christabel's father, who has quarrelled with him. But this is not true, because she is in fact an evil spirit in the form of Geraldine. This poem is one of the most beautiful in English. Among the more noticeable lines are the following, which refer to the quarrel:

> And constancy[A] lives in realms[B] above;
> And life is thorny; and youth is vain;
> And to be wroth[C] with one we love
> Doth work like madness in the brain.
>
> [A] faithfulness   [B] kingdoms   [C] angry

Once when Coleridge was staying in Devon, he fell asleep while reading in *Purchas his Pilgrims* (see page 30) about Kubla Khan's great building in Xanadu. On waking he knew that he had dreamed several hundred poetic lines on the subject, and he began at once to write them down. Unluckily he was interrupted, and was never again able to remember the rest:

> In Xanadu did Kubla Khan
> A stately[A] pleasure dome[B] decree[C],
> Where Alph, the sacred river ran,
> Through caverns[D] measureless to man
> Down to a sunless sea.
>
> [A] proud [B] building [C] order [D] caves

The buildings were set among gardens, rivers and forests, and caves of ice. All this is described in words which produce a strange and magic picture.

Wordsworth's part in the *Lyrical Ballads* was more difficult to perform successfully than Coleridge's; for he had to make ordinary things seem wonderful. He wrote more than half the book, and his love of nature is immediately clear. In *Lines Written above Tintern Abbey*, the poet returns to a scene of his boyhood, sits under a tree, and looks at the lovely views which he used to remember when far away:

> But oft in lonely rooms and 'mid[A] the din[B]
> Of towns and cities, I have owed to them
> In hours of weariness[C], sensations[D] sweet,
> Felt in the blood, and felt along the heart.
>
> [A] among [B] noise [C] tiredness [D] feelings

Among his best sonnets are *Westminster Bridge,* an emotional view of London asleep, and *London,* 1802. The latter is a cry for help in the troubles of the world: 'Milton, thou shouldst be living at this hour. England hath need of thee'. Well known among other short poems are *The Daffodils, The Solitary Reaper,* and *Lucy.*

The *Ode on Intimations of Immortality*[3] (1807) is longer and more important. The poet finds a basis of faith in memories of childhood, before the business of the world has shut off the view of heaven:

[3] *intimations of immortality,* signs leading one to expect a life without end after the present life.

> Shades of the prison-house[A] begin to close
>   Upon the growing boy,
> But he beholds[B] the light, and whence[C] it flows,
>   He sees it in his joy
>
> [A] (the world)   [B] sees   [C] from where

In the same poem Wordsworth expresses his belief in the idea that, as well as going to a life without end, we come from another life:

> Our birth is but a sleep and a forgetting:
> The soul that rises with us, our life's star,
> Hath had elsewhere its setting,
> And cometh from afar:
> Not in entire forgetfulness,
> And not in utter[A] nakedness[B],
>   But trailing[C] clouds of glory do we come
>   From God, who is our home.
>
> [A] complete   [B] bareness   [C] pulling

The Prelude, a record in fourteen books of verse of Wordworth's own progress in poetry and thought, was written during the years 1799-1805. In it he remembers his schooldays, his time at Cambridge, his visits to London and France, and his life in France during the Revolution. *The Excursion* (1814), in nine books, is the middle part of a great philosophical work which he planned but never completed.

GEORGE GORDON, LORD BYRON, was a romantic figure, but his poetry was much influenced by the classical form of Pope. Byron dressed splendidly, went to fight for the freedom of Greece, satirized many sides of English life, and hated all false and insincere talk. He died of fever at Missolonghi (Mesolongion, in western Greece), but his body was brought home to England for burial.

Byron's poetry, though powerful, lacks the finest poetic imagination. His words mean only what they say, and have no further magic. Though he was influenced by the eighteenth century, his satires lack Pope's polished perfection and command of words. His verse possesses neither Wordworth's power of suggestion, nor Coleridge's mystery; but, except when he wrote carelessly, it is often strong and beautiful.

Childe Harold (1809-17), written in the Spenserian stanza, tells the story of a man who goes off to travel far and wide because he is disgusted with life's foolish pleasures. (The man is, in fact, Lord Byron.) The different places that he visits give the poet an opportunity to describe what once happened in them. Thus, in Belgium, the poet remembers the recent battle of Waterloo and the officers' dance that took place in Brussels just before it:

> There was a sound of revelry[A] by night,
> And Belgium's capital had gathered then
> Her beauty and her chivalry[B], and bright
> The lamps shone o'er fair women and brave men.
> A thousand hearts beat happily; and when
> Music arose with its voluptuous[C] swell,
> Soft eyes looked love to eyes which spake again,
> And all went merry as a marriage bell.
> But hush[D]! Hark[E]! A deep sound strikes like a rising knell[F].

[A] enjoyment   [B] brave officers   [C] giving pleasure   [D] be silent   [E] listen
[F] slow, sad ringing of a bell

In 1812 and the following years Byron wrote several narrative poems about the East. In *The Giaour* [= the Christian] (1813) a slave, Leila, is thrown into the sea by her master Hassan. In revenge her lover, the Giaour, kills Hassan. *The Bride of Abydos* (1813) is a tragic love story. *The Corsair* and *Lara* (1814), both in heroic couplets, are stories of love, fighting and death.

Don Juan (1818-24), a long poem of astonishing adventure, is also a satire which attacks some of Byron's enemies. It starts with a shipwreck, and continues with its later results; but the main story is often left so that the poet may put forward ideas on various subjects. It contains the beautiful lyric which begins as follows:

> The isles of Greece, the isles of Greece,
> Where burning Sappho loved and sung,
> Where grew the arts of war and peace,
>   Where Delos rose and Phoebus sprung.

Byron wrote a number of short poems which are popular. *The Assyrian Came Down* is learnt at school. His plays are not very good, but his poetry was popular because he attacked false ideas, and because the eastern scene was unusual in his time. He could give memorable form to ideas that were already in his readers' minds:

> Man's love is of man's life a thing apart,
> 'T is woman's whole existence. (DON JUAN)

and he makes us laugh with his sharp satire – sometimes using intentionally bad rhymes:

> But – Oh! ye lords of ladies intellectual[A],
> Inform us truly, have they not hen-pecked[B] you all?
>
> [A] interested in things of the mind
> [B] ruled by continuous complaints   (DON JUAN)

but he very seldom takes us to the stars.

Percy Bysshe Shelley drawn by Soord

PERCY BYSSHE SHELLEY was a greater poet, of good family, restless, and rich. He struggled against the causes of human misery and against accepted religions. He saw goodness in the whole of nature, and he wanted all men to be free. His first important poem, *Alastor, or The Spirit of Solitude*[4] (1816) is in blank verse and shows Wordsworth's influence. It expresses joy in the universe and sorrow for the violent feelings of men. *The Revolt of Islam* (1818) is a cry of impatience at the cruelty of the world, but it is too long (5,000 lines). The reader's love of freedom is dulled by too much language, and the poem is written in the Spenserian stanza, which is not suitable. *The Cenci* (1819), a shocking but honest tragedy, has some dramatic power. *Prometheus Unbound* (1820), another play (on the Greek model), deals with the human struggle against the power of false gods. The argument is dull, but the lyrics are beautiful.

Adonais (1821), one of his best poems, is an elegy on the death of Keats. One of his finest sonnets, *Ozymandias*, expresses the uselessness and the shortness of all earthly power. His lyrics are among the best in the language, and include *The Cloud* (I bring fresh showers for the thirsting flowers), *To a Skylark* (Hail to thee, blithe[5] spirit), *The Indian Serenade* and *Stanzas Written in Dejection*[6] *near Naples*. The famous *Ode to the West Wind* gives expression to his wild and free imagination:

> If I were a dead leaf thou mightest bear;
> If I were a swift[A] cloud to fly with thee;
> A wave to pant[B] beneath thy power, and share
> The impulse[C] of thy strength, only less free
> Than thou, O uncontrollable! If even
> I were as in my boyhood, and could be
> The comrade[D] of thy wandering under heaven!

[A] fast   [B] breathe heavily   [C] driving power   [D] companion

Shelley loved the wild wind, but JOHN KEATS loved beauty and rest. A friend in 1813 gave him Spenser's *Faerie Queene* to read, and this awoke his poetic powers. He studied the poets and he studied nature

---

[4] *solitude*, being alone.

[5] *blithe*, joyful (like the song of the high-flying *skylark*).

[6] *dejection*, great sadness.

John Keats who lived from 1795-1821 drawn by his close companion C. A. Brown

too. He could write lines in Wordsworth's manner, but with more music, such lines as 'A little noiseless noise among the leaves.'

His early poem *Endymion* (1818), in four books, is based on old ideas: the old gods, the love of the moon-goddess for a shepherd, Venus and Adonis, Glaucus and Scylla. It was violently criticized, but he did not lose faith in himself. In 1820 he published *Lamia* (in which a snake is changed into a beautiful girl). *Isabella* was in the same book. It is taken from a story in Boccaccio's *Decameron*. Isabella is the daughter of a proud family of Florence (Firenze). Lorenzo falls in love with her, and her brothers kill him. She finds his buried body and puts his head in a flower-pot. Her brothers notice that she spends a lot of time with this pot, and they steal it. When they find the head in it, they feel guilty and escape. *The Eve of Saint Agnes*, which belongs to this time also, is based on the idea that on that night girls may see their lovers in dreams.

Hyperion (1818-9) was never finished. Hyperion is the old sun-god. The young Apollo, god of music and poetry and the sun, is introduced, but there the poem ends. It contains several examples of the stillness in some of Keats's poetry:

> No stir of air was there
> Not so much life as on a summer's day
> Robs not one light seed from the feathered grass,
> But where the dead leaf fell, there did it rest.
>
> And still they were the same bright, patient stars.

The same effects may be found in his *Ode on a Grecian Urn*[7] (1819), a description of the figures on its side, which will never move:

> Heard melodies[A] are sweet, but those unheard
> Are sweeter.
>
> Fair youth beneath the trees, thou canst not leave
> Thy song, nor ever can those trees be bare.
> Bold lover, never, never, canst thou kiss.
>
> When old age shall this generation[B] waste
> Thou shalt remain, in midst[C] of other woe[D]
> Than ours, a friend to man, to whom thou sayest,
> 'Beauty is truth, truth beauty' – that is all
> Ye know on earth, and all ye need to know.
>
> [A] music   [B] people of one age   [C] middle   [D] sorrow

Other great odes written at about the same time are *To a Nightingale* (My heart aches) and *To Autumn* (Season of mists). He wrote more than twenty sonnets. One of the best is *On First Looking into Chapman's Homer* (Oft have I travelled).

Keats wrote poetry of rich detail and accused Shelley of using language which was too thin. Keats also wrote a good ballad, *La Belle Dame Sans Merci*[8], in which a knight dreams of his lady, but wakes alone on a cold hillside, 'where no birds sing.' 'La Belle Dame' is supposed by some to be tuberculosis, a disease which killed Keats at the early age of twenty-six. Shelley, too, died young; he was drowned near Lerici, Italy, at the age of twenty-nine. Byron also died (of fever) before he was forty.

A less important poet of the time was ROBERT SOUTHEY. He wrote an immense amount of prose and verse. His poems often told a story, and were set in far-away lands. Among the shorter poems are *The Inchcape Rock* and *The Battle of Blenheim*. His prose *Life of Nelson* is well known.

THOMAS CAMPBELL produced some battle poems which are full of spirit, such as *Ye Mariners*[9] *of England* and *The Battle of the Baltic*.

---

[7] *Grecian urn*, a vessel (for liquids or ashes) made by the ancient Greeks.

[8] (French) The beautiful lady without mercy.

[9] *mariners*, sailors.

A picture of Ludgate Hill by Gustave Doré showing St. Paul's Cathedral in the background

Chapter Ten

Later nineteenth-century poets

The early poems of ALFRED, LORD TENNYSON were much criticized, but in his later books he rewrote some and omitted others altogether. His *Poems, Chiefly Lyrical* (1830) and *Poems* (1833) were an improvement, though they were still the work of a young man. The music is there already, but the thought is not deep. *The Lotos Easters*, a poem on the wanderings of Ulysses and his men, gives a taste of the rhythm of which Tennyson was a master:

> Surely, surely slumber[A] is more sweet than toil[B], the shore
> Than labour[B] on the deep mid-ocean, wind and wave and oar!
> Oh rest ye, brother mariners[C]; we will not wander more.
>
> [A] sleep   [B] hard work   [C] sailors

Tennyson knew well that more thought was needed in great work, and in 1842 he published two books of poems which are serious and thoughtful as well as musical. The rhythm is still there, and Fitzgerald thought that Tennyson never wrote better poems than these; but today many people prefer *The Idylls*[1] *of the King*.

Tennyson had become a very careful artist, choosing each word and its exact place with close attention. In *Morte D'Arthur* he put Malory's story into blank verse in which the magic voice may clearly be heard:

[1] *idyll*, descriptive poem.

Part of an illustration from Tennyson's poem The Idylls of the King showing Guinevere and Lancelot

So all day long the noise of battle rolled
Among the mountains by the winter sea,
Until King Arthur's table, man by man,
Had fallen in Lyonesse[A] about their lord
King Arthur.

[A] Lyonesse was a land which is now supposed to lie beneath the sea to the south-west of England

The Idylls of the King included this short poem and others on the same story: *Enid, Vivien, Elaine,* and *Guinevere* appeared in 1859, and others in 1869, 1871-2, and 1885. *The Passing of Arthur* describes at the end how Sir Bedivere places the wounded king in the ship which is carrying the queen (see page 19). Sir Bedivere, in sorrow because of the end of the Round Table and the death of the other knights, asks what he can do now:

And slowly answered Arthur from the barge[A],
'The old order changeth, yielding place to new,
And God fulfils[B] himself in many ways
Lest one good custom should corrupt[C] the world.
Comfort thyself! What comfort is in me?
I have lived my life, and that which I have done
May He within himself make pure! But thou,
If thou shouldst never see my face again,
Pray for my soul'.

[A] ship   [B] reaches his aim   [C] ruin

Tennyson used many metres and made experiments with new ones. For example, he tried hexameters,[2] like Clough; and he was fond of the four-line stanza rhyming abba:

Yet waft[A] me from the harbour mouth,
    Wild wind, I seek[B] a warmer sky
    And I will see before I die
The palms[C] and temples of the south.

[A] blow   [B] search for   [C] tall trees which grow in hot countries

This is also the metre that he used for his long poem *In Memoriam* (1833-50), an elegy for his friend Hallam, who died in Vienna at the early age of 22. Though the poem has its fine qualities, it is too long for a discussion of death alone, and the sorrow for the loss of a friend gradually changes into an expression of a wider love of God and man.

In general Tennyson's shorter poems are better than the long ones. *Ulysses* (1842) expresses in fine lines the leader's decision to 'sail beyond the sunset and the baths Of all the western stars until I die.' *The Princess* (1847 and 1853) contains fine lyrics; here is a verse of one which has been set to music:

Sweet and low, sweet and low,
    Wind of the western sea.
Low, low, breathe and blow,

[2] *hexameter*, a metre used for heroic verse by the ancient Greek and Latin poets but difficult to write well in English; the line has six feet, strictly controlled in form by old custom.

Wind of the western sea!
Over the rolling waters go,
Come from the dying moon and blow,
    Blow him again to me;
While my little one, while my pretty one, sleeps.

Tennyson's plays are not important. The best is *Becket* (1884) on the subject of the quarrel between King Henry II and Thomas à Becket, who was murdered at Canterbury in 1170. Chaucer's pilgrims were on their way to Becket's grave, and T. S. Eliot has written a play on this murder.

Tennyson's influence in his own time was immense. He reflected the changing ideas of his age in his various poems; but at the beginning of the twentieth century, his popularity fell.

ROBERT BROWNING was unlike Tennyson. For Browning the intellect[3] was, from the beginning, more important than the music. This made him popular in universities after his death. He did not reflect very much the ideas of his time; he did not go to an ancient university. His immense knowledge came from his studies in London, his travels and his own work. He was hopeful by nature and often attempted poems beyond his powers. In 1846 he married Elizabeth Barrett, one of England's greatest poetesses, against her father's wishes and in spite of her bad health. They went to live in Italy at Florence, a place which influenced the work of both.

Browning's *Pauline* (1833), containing more than 1,000 lines, is only part of a much longer poem that he planned but never wrote. He tried writing plays without much success. His tragedy *Strafford* (1837) ran for only a few nights in London. Plays, as we have seen, must have a carefully built structure, and must contain action, but Browning's gift was more in poetry. He had more success with dramatic material for one speaker.

Sordello (1840) is his most difficult poem. It is a story of events in 1200 and its details are complicated. It has been said that neither the first line (Who will, may hear Sordello's story told), nor the last line (Who would, has heard Sordello's story told) is true.

One of his successful dramatic poems is *Pippa Passes* (1841). In this a girl, Pippa, wanders through the town singing, and her song

[3] *intellect*, the power of reasoning and understanding.

influences people who (unknown to her) hear it. Part of it is as cheerful as Browning himself:

> The year's at the spring
> The day's at the morn;
> Morning's at seven ...
> All's right with the world.

The poems in *Dramatic Lyrics* (1842) and *Dramatic Romances* (1845) are a great advance on Browning's dramas. *The Pied Piper of Hamelin*, a poem in the second of these books, described the removal of rats from a city by a musician whose music leads them away. There is some difficulty when he goes for his agreed pay, ('A thousand guilders! Come, take fifty!') and so he leads the children away like the rats, and they all disappear into a hill.

Robert Browning and his wife Elizabeth Barrett Browning

Browning's difficult style is the result of his unusual knowledge of
words and his bold ways of building sentences. *Rabbi ben Ezra,* in
Dramatis Personae (1864), gives something of Browning's philosophy.
It contains the line:

> Irks care the crop-full bird? Frets doubt the maw-crammed
> beast?

This difficult pair of questions would be written by another author
as 'Does care irk (trouble) a bird whose stomach is full? Does doubt
fret (trouble, worry) the beast whose stomach is full? No.'

Browning had a neat way of expressing ideas. A few examples may
be interesting:

> That shall be tomorrow,
> Not tonight.
> I must bury sorrow
> Out of sight.   (A WOMAN'S LAST WORD)

> Oh, to be in England
> Now that April's there.   (HOME THOUGHTS FROM ABROAD)

> Nobly, nobly Cape Saint Vincent to the north west died away;
> Sunset ran, one glorious blood-red, reeking ᴬ into Cadiz Bay
> ᴬ like smoke   (HOME THOUGHTS FROM THE SEA)

> Who knows but the world may end tonight?
>   (THE LAST RIDE TOGETHER)

> Never the time and the place
> And the loved one all together!
>   (NEVER THE TIME AND THE PLACE)

The Ring and the Book (1868-9) is a poem based on a book that he
found in Florence. This is the 'Book' of the title. It is an old story of
the murder of a wife, Pompilia, by her husband, told in various
ways by different people, who do not always have the same view of
the details.

On the day of Browning's death a volume, *Asolando,* was published
which contained many fine poems including the following lines:

One who never turned his back, but marched breast[A] forward,
Never doubted clouds would break,
Never dreamed, though right were worsted[B], wrong would
     triumph[C],
Held[D] we fall to rise, are baffled[E] to fight better,
     Sleep to wake.

[A] chest   [B] beaten   [C] succeed   [D] believed   [E] puzzled

Tennyson and Browning were the two greatest poetic figures of their time, but there were other great poets. WALTER SAVAGE LANDOR was chiefly a writer of prose, but some of his verse is important. A few lines that he wrote at the end of a long life easily find room in the memory:

I strove[A] with none, for none was worth my strife;
     Nature I loved, and next to nature, art.
I warmed both hands before the fire of life;
     It sinks, and I am ready to depart[B].

[A] struggled   [B] go away

MATTHEW ARNOLD, the son of Dr Arnold, headmaster of Rugby, wrote a poem on the school, *Rugby Chapel* (1867) ('Coldly, sadly descends the autumn evening'). Arnold was weighed down by the problems of his time, and much of his work is sad. *Thyrsis* (1867) is a lament [4] for his friend, Clough. *The Scholar Gipsy* [5] (1853) tells of an Oxford man who joins a band of gipsies and wanders with them. There are good descriptions of the country, but Arnold's anxieties appear once more:

This strange disease of modern life
With its sick hurry and divided aims.

He was unable to find rest, and greatly admired Wordsworth's calmness. He made a fine collection of Wordsworth's poetry; his sad

---

[4] *lament,* an expression of deep sorrow, usually at the death of a loved person.
[5] *gipsy,* a member of a race of wanderers; they are of Indian origin but have lived in western Europe for 400 years.

Memorial Verses (1850) are a lament for that poet's death, and for the deaths of other poets at home and abroad:

> Goethe[A] in Weimar sleeps, and Greece
> Long since saw Byron's struggle cease[B].
> But one such death remained to come:
> The last poetic voice is dumb[C]
> We stand today by Wordsworth's tomb[D].
>
> [A] German poet, 1749-1832   [B] end   [C] silent   [D] grave

Arnold wrote a critical sonnet on Shakespeare, whom he praised too much. One of his other poems, *Empedocles on Etna,* has been highly praised, perhaps because it is not altogether sad.

ARTHUR HUGH CLOUGH, Arnold's friend, wrote a few important poems. Some of his early work, such as *Easter Day, Naples* (1849) is good. *Say not the struggle naught availeth* [= Do not say the struggle is useless] is a cry of encouragement. You may seem to be failing, he says, but perhaps your unseen friends are winning the battle:

> And not by eastern windows only
>   When daylight comes, comes in the light;
> In front, the sun climbs slow – how slowly!
>   But westward, look! The land is bright!

Clough's *Amours de Voyage* (1849) (= Loves when travelling) is a

*Title page drawing by her brother Dante Gabriel Rossetti to
Christina Rossetti's collection of poems entitled Goblin Market*

taste of more modern poetry before its time. Like another of his poems, it is written in hexameters, common in Latin but not in English; and he writes in a conversational way:

> T´iber is b´eautiful t´oo, and the ´orchard^A sl´opes and the ´Anio
> F´alling, f´alling y´et, to the ´ancient l´yrical c´adence^B.

^A fruit-garden   ^B falling sound

The sonnets of DANTE GABRIEL ROSSETTI are among the most musical in English. Rossetti was a painter as well as a poet, and his poems have been criticized as belonging to the 'Fleshly School' of poetry. But he replied that poetry ought to be based on the senses. Many of his lines are clearly written by a man with a painter's eye:

> She had a mouth made to bring death to life.
>
> (A LAST CONFESSION)
>
> You have been mine before, –
> How long ago I may not know:
> But just when at the swallow's soar^A
>   Your neck turned so,
> Some veil did fall. I knew it all of yore^B

^A bird's flying up   ^B in old times   (SUDDEN LIGHT)

> This is that lady beauty, in whose praise
> Thy voice and hand shake still – long known to thee
> By flying hair and fluttering hem^A – the beat
> Following her daily of thy heart and feet.

^A waving edge   (SOUL'S BEAUTY)

The pictures of the mouth and the neck and of the flying hair and the fluttering hem of the dress are what a painter sees.

Rossetti wrote about nature with his eye on it, but he did not feel it in his bones as Wordsworth does; he studied it. Rossetti was too fond of alliteration; notice 'flying hair and fluttering hem'.

His sister, CHRISTINA GEORGINA ROSSETTI wrote mostly sad and religious poems and poems for the young. Among her best productions are her excellent sonnets on unhappy love.

Another great poetess of this time was Elizabeth Barrett, who, on her marriage, became ELIZABETH BARRETT BROWNING. Some of her poems are too long, but in a sonnet she could not write too much because the form is limited to fourteen lines. Thus much of her best work is contained in *Sonnets from the Portuguese* (1850). She pretended at first that these sonnets were translated from the Portuguese; they were really an entirely original expression of her love for Robert Browning:

> How do I love thee? Let me count the ways.
> I love thee to the depth and breadth and height
> My soul can reach.

Her marriage to Browning is the subject of a play by Besier, *The Barretts of Wimpole Street*, (1930).

ALGERNON CHARLES SWINBURNE was a follower of Dante Gabriel Rossetti, and misused alliteration more than Rossetti did. He wrote much political verse, but his new rich music was first heard in his drama *Atalanta in Calydon*. Here is an example of its verse:

> Maiden[A] and mistress[B] of the months and stars
> Now folded in the flowerless fields of heaven.
> [A] girl   [B] lady

Swinburne's poetry has been criticized for lack of thought; but the singing is splendid. He was much blamed for moral reasons when *Poems and Ballads* appeared in 1866. A later book of *Poems and Ballads* (1878), which gave less offence, shows his interest in French writers, and includes the laments for Baudelaire and Théophile Gautier, and the translations of Villon's *Ballades*.

Tristram of Lyonesse (1882), usually considered to be his best work, tells the undying story of Tristram and Iseult. Tristram went to Ireland to bring the beautiful Iseult to marry King Mark of Cornwall, but fell in love with her himself. Yet he did his duty, and she married the king. Tristram went to Britanny, and there he married the other Iseult, Iseult of the White Hand, daughter of the Duke of Brittany. The story is not always the same. In the version used by Swinburne, Tristram lay dying in Brittany and sent a message to

A painting of Swinburne in 1865 by George Frederick Watts

his old love in Cornwall. Queen Iseult then set out to go to him; but Tristram was told that the ship, when it was seen, had a black sail. This was a sign that she was not on board, and he died of sorrow. Swinburne wrote his poem in couplets, with his usual alliteration:

> Nor shall they feel or fear, whose date is done,
> Aught[A] that made once more dark the living sun
> And bitterer in their breathing lips the breath
> Than the dark dawn[B] and bitter dust of death.

[A] anything [B] break of day

The volume containing *Tristram* also contained his sonnets on the Elizabethan dramatists. Swinburne wrote plays, but they are not of great value.

One of the greatest poetic translators was EDWARD FITZGERALD He translated six of Calderon's plays (1853), the *Agamemnon* of Aeschylus (1876) and (most important) the *Rubaiyat* [= Four-line verses] of the Persian poet Omar Khayyam. Most translations lose something and are not as good as the originals; but this book (1859) is considered by some Persian scholars to be better than Omar Khayyam's work. Fitzgerald did not stick too closely to his originals, but gave the general sense. In his translation of the *Rubaiyat,* he entirely omitted the hidden meanings of the original (in which, for example, the wine meant God). The suggestion of the whole poem is, 'Eat, drink and be merry, for tomorrow we die,' and the effect on the thoughtful mind is therefore that of sad music:

> Ah, make the most of what ye yet may spend
> Before we too into the dust descend;
>   Dust into dust, and under dust, to lie
> Sans[A] wine, sans song, sans singer and – sans end!

[A] without

As the nineteenth century drew near its end Meredith the novelist was writing a few good poems. *Juggling Jerry* gives a brave old man's view of the nearness of death. *The Lark Ascending* has a music which reminds the reader very slightly of Milton's *L'Allegro*. RUDYARD KIPLING was another novelist who wrote poems. These are in the language of ordinary men, strong and free. They concern men who are or were in unusual conditions and strange places. Those who go home still have memories of persons and places far away, and Kipling put their thoughts into words. In *Mandalay* he gives the thoughts of a British soldier who has left the bright East and gone back to London:

> By the old Moulmein Pagoda, looking eastward to the sea,
> There's a Burma girl a-sitting, and I know she thinks of me.
> For the wind is in the palm-trees[A], and the temple-bells
>   they say:
> 'Come you back, you British soldier; come you back to
>   Mandalay!' ...
> But that's all shove[B] behind me – long ago and far away,
> And there ain't[C] no buses running from the Bank to
>   Mandalay.
> [A] tall trees that grow in hot countries   [B] pushed   [C] aren't

The first book of poems published by FRANCIS THOMPSON appeared in 1893, and included the famous *Hound of Heaven*. Other books of his came out in 1895 and 1897.

A fair number of other poets wrote at the end of the nineteenth and the beginning of the twentieth centuries, but these are best considered in a later chapter.

George Eliot was the pen-name of Mary-Anne Evans, one of the greatest nineteenth-century novelists

Chapter Eleven

Nineteenth-century novelists

Though JANE AUSTEN wrote her books in troubled years which included the French revolution, her novels are calm pictures of society life. She understood the importance of the family in human affairs and, though two of her brothers were in the navy[1], she paid little attention to the violence of nations.

The title given to her first novel was *Elinor and Marianne* (1795), but this was later rewritten and published as *Sense and Sensibility*[2] (1811). In 1796 she started *First Impressions*[3], which was later published as *Pride and Prejudice*[4] (1813). *Mansfield Park* appeared in 1814 and *Emma* in 1816. *Northanger Abbey*[5] (1818) was begun as a satire on Mrs Radcliffe's *Mysteries of Udolpho*, and to show that real life is very different. *Persuasion* (1818) was published in the same year. It is her last novel, and there is a belief that her own love affairs are reflected in those of Anne Elliot.

Jane Austen brought the novel of family life to its highest point of perfection. Her works were untouched by the ugliness of the outside world; she kept the action to scenes familiar to her through her own experience. Her first novels were refused by publishers, and she had to wait fifteen or twenty years after beginning to write before any novel was accepted. *Northanger Abbey* was sold to a bookseller in

---

[1] *navy*, a country's warships.
[2] *sensibility*, readiness to be influenced by fine feelings.
[3] *impressions*, effects on the mind.
[4] *prejudice*, unreasonable feeling against something.
[5] *abbey*, religious building.

Bath for ten pounds, but he did not publish it, and it was bought back later on.

Her knowledge, within her own limits, was deep and true; but her performance in writing these novels was astonishing. She manages her characters with a master's touch. Miss Bates in *Emma*, though herself uninteresting, is not allowed to destroy the reader's interest. Elizabeth Bennet in *Pride and Prejudice* is quite as delightful as Jane Austen called her. Mr Bennet is nearly as delightful, and most of the other leading characters in this novel are first-class literary creations. A general remark is the amusing first sentence of the book:

> It is a truth universally acknowledged [recognised]
> that a single man in possession of a good fortune must
> be in want of a wife.

An illustration from Jane Austen's last novel Persuasion

Then we are taken straight into a conversation between the talkative Mrs Bennet and her more silent husband. In a few lines we know them; when she tells him excitedly about the new arrival at the largest house in the neighbourhood, we are not surprised at his question:

> 'Is he married or single?'
>
> 'Oh! single, my dear, to be sure! A single man of large fortune; four or five thousand a year. What a fine thing for our girls!'
>
> 'How-so? how can it affect them?'
>
> 'My dear Mr Bennet,' replied his wife, 'how can you be so tiresome.[A] You must know that I am thinking of his marrying one of them.'
>
> 'Is that his design[B] in settling here?'
>
> [A] annoying   [B] purpose

In general the least attractive of Jane Austen's characters are the young men.

MARY SHELLEY, the poet's wife, is remembered now chiefly as the writer of a famous novel of terror, *Frankenstein* (1818). It was published in the year that saw *Northanger Abbey*, a satire on this sort of novel. *Frankenstein* was begun as a ghost story; but Mrs Shelley finally made her character, the Genevan student Frankenstein, collect bones, build a human being, and give it life. Everyone hates it for its ugliness, and it is lonely and fierce. It murders Frankenstein's brother and his wife. Frankenstein follows it to the far north and is himself killed by it. The creature then disappears. It has remained the pattern of machine-men, and the book may well be considered as the first attempt at science fiction[6], a form of literature very common in the modern world. Mrs Shelley also wrote *The Last Man* (1826) the story of the slow destruction by disease of every member (except one) of the human race.

Though EDGAR ALLAN POE was born in the United States, he went to school near London. Most of his poems were unsuccessful, but his stories have filled thousands with interest and fear. Under

[6] *fiction*, stories in which the characters and events are imaginary.

the title, *Tales of Mystery and Imagination*, they include *The Fall of the House of Usher* (1839), *The Masque of the Red Death* (1842), *A Descent into the Maelstrom* [7] (1841), *The Mystery of Marie Roget* (1842) and *The Murders in the Rue Morgue* (1841). Poe's powerful descriptions of astonishing and unusual events have the attraction of terrible things.

Before he turned to the historical novel, SIR WALTER SCOTT wrote verse – a kind of verse which formed for him a suitable introduction to the prose that he wrote later. It is historical verse and may well be considered here. *The Lay of the Last Minstrel* (1805), in irregular stanzas, is based on an old Scottish story and includes some good ballads. A few lines from this poem will show Scott's verse style:

> Breathes there a man with soul so dead
> Who never to himself hath said,
>   'This is my own, my native land'?
> Whose heart hath ne'er within him burned
> As home his footsteps he hath turned,
> From wandering on a foreign strand? [A]
>   [A] shore

Another verse tale of love and fighting, *Marmion* (1808), includes a description of Flodden Field, a battle between Scots and English in 1513. *The Lady of the Lake* (1810) is also based on fighting and love; and *The Lord of the Isles* (1815) tells in verse the story of Robert Bruce.

Scott soon discovered that he could not write poetry as good as Byron's, and so he turned away from it; but as a historical novelist he has no rival. He read the older novelists, and himself began to write *Waverley* in 1805. It appeared in 1814, and for the next eighteen years Scott wrote novel after novel. In 1826 he lost all his money through the business failure of his publisher and printer. He owed £100,000, but refused the money with which his friends offered to help him. He sat down to pay the immense debt by writing, but died before he could do so. In spite of that, his books brought in enough money after his death to pay the last pound.

[7] *Maelstrom*, a part of the sea off the coast of Norway where a spinning effect of the tides was supposed to suck ships down to destruction.

The modern world is very different from Scott's world. It does not admire glory in battle as much as the men of Scott's day, partly because there are so many other dangerous events to remember. Space-travel is more exciting to us than fighting with swords. These facts have lessened the attraction of Scott's novels; yet we must admire his powers of description. His characters, especially the unusual ones, are well drawn. His historical studies were long and deep, and his stories have the force of careful detail. He has left so much that few people can read all of it.

Among the well-known novels, *Waverley* goes back only to the eighteenth century for its story, and the next two books, *Guy Mannering* (1815) and *The Antiquary*[8] (1816), are laid in the time of Scott's own youth. But in *Old Mortality* (1816), he put the scene at the end of the seventeenth century. Among other novels about early times, he wrote *Ivanhoe* (1819), *Kenilworth* (1821), *Quentin Durward* (1823), *The Talisman*[9] (1825), *Woodstock* (1826), and *The Fair Maid of Perth* (1828). He wrote a number of dramas, which are not important; and several books of criticism, such as *The Works of Dryden* and *The Works of Swift*. He also produced essays, and a *Life of Napoleon Buonaparte* (1827); yet these form only a small part of his various publications.

Scott is rather difficult to read, especially in those places where his characters speak dialect[10]. Though the stories themselves are good, the books are long for the modern reader. His hard work and his knowledge of history continually astonish the reader; yet the love interest in the stories often lacks depth, and his heroes and heroines – especially the heroines – are weak when compared with the violent scenes in which they live. Scott's style is sometimes heavy and much influenced by the old and flowery ways of speech. But he loved people, as Chaucer and Shakespeare did, and he could tell stories well.

The sea stories of FREDERICK MARRYAT were after the style of Smollett's novels, but they were gentler. In *Peter Simple* (1834), perhaps his best book, a foolish son is sent to sea and meets some foolish adventures; but he shows himself a brave officer, is taken

---

[8] *antiquary*, one who studies ancient things.
[9] *talisman*, something which produces astonishing effects.
[10] *dialect*, special language of one district.

prisoner, wins a beautiful wife, and so on. Chucks, a character in the book, amuses everyone by beginning his angry speeches politely and ending them in rough language. Another novel about the sea is *Mr Midshipman*[11] *Easy* (1836), in which the hero also goes to sea; but Jack Easy has a firm belief that all men are equal, and on board ship this idea causes a number of difficulties.

At about the same time EDWARD BULWER LYTTON (LORD LYTTON) was writing novels in a style rather like Scott's. He had to support himself by his literary work, so that it is a good thing that he was poor. One of his best remembered books, *The Last Days of Pompeii* (1834), made a good film in the early days and the book is on the whole a fine piece of writing. *The Last of the Barons* (1843) and *Harold* (1848) are also important.

CHARLES DICKENS is generally considered to be one of the greatest English novelists, and he is one of the few whose works did not become unpopular after his death. He began with *Pickwick* (1836-7), which came out in parts and gave English literature some of its most charming and amusing characters. Mr Pickwick himself is almost too kind to be true; it is fortunate for him that he meets and employs the cheerful Sam Weller to keep him out of most of the trouble caused by his own kindness, or to comfort him with words of wisdom when the trouble has not been avoided:

> 'It's over, and can't be helped, and that's one consolation[A], as they always says in Turkey, ven[B] they cuts the wrong man's head off.'
>
> [A] comfort after misfortune [B] when

None of the members of the Pickwick Club could be described as wise in the ways of the world, but to go through life without meeting them in Dickens's pages would be a great loss.

Twice Dickens wrote historical novels, *Barnaby Rudge* (1841) and *A Tale of Two Cities* (1849), a story of the French Revolution and of events in London at the same time. Sometimes his novels were written partly with the purpose of improving social conditions. *Oliver Twist* (1837-8), the story of a poor boy's cruel treatment and

[11] *midshipman*, officer of low rank.

An illustration by Phiz from Charles Dickens' Pickwick Papers

miserable adventures, includes descriptions of hunger, stealing, murder and hanging. *A Christmas Carol*[12] (1843) is the story of a bad character who improves his behaviour after a ghost tells him the manner of his death. *Hard Times* (1854) is set in industrial surroundings, where Gradgrind's children are brought up among hard facts and without any help for the spirit. The son robs a bank, and the girl makes an unhappy marriage; but luckily the father suddenly understands his own foolishness.

[12] *carol*, song.

David Copperfield (1849-50) is based on Dickens's own life, which had a sad beginning. It is one of the most popular of his novels, but it cannot be called cheerful. *Nicholas Nickleby* (1838-9) is the tale of a boy who is left poor on his father's death. He is sent to work in a school, Dotheboys Hall [=Do-The-Boys], where the master, Squeers, treats forty miserable pupils cruelly, and teaches them nothing. Nicholas gives the reader a good deal of pleasure when he gives the criminal Squeers a good beating, and then escapes.

All these novels are crowded with characters, either fully developed or drawn by a few quick but sure strokes of the great writer's pen. The reader of modern English novels or newspapers will not get far without finding mention – in a way which supposes that the reader needs no other explanation – of the name of a minor[13] character from one of the books listed above, or reference, for example, to the evil Quilp, the great-hearted Mrs Jarley, or honest Kit Nubbles *(The Old Curiosity Shop)*; to Mr Pecksniff, Mark Tapley, or the wicked Mrs Gamp *(Martin Chuzzlewit)*; to Mrs Jellyby, Jo the crossing sweeper, or Chadband *(Bleak House)*; to kind, strong Joe Gargery, the dishonest Pumblechook, Mr Jaggers the clever lawyer, his good-hearted clerk Wemmick, or Wemmick's 'Aged Parent' *(Great Expectations)*; and so on.

Dickens's prose varies in quality, but he is nearly always readable. In his different novels he describes and attacks many kinds of unpleasant people and places – bad schools and schoolmasters, government departments, bad prisons, dirty houses. His characters include thieves, murderers, men in debt, stupid and unwashed men and women, hungry children, and those who do their best to deceive the honest. Although many of his scenes are terribly unpleasant, he usually keeps the worst descriptions out of his books; therefore the reader does not throw the book into the fire, but continues to read. Some of his gentler characters are very weak; some of the sad situations that he describes are too miserable to be true. He uses too much black paint. But he wanted to raise kindness and goodness in men's hearts, and he used tears and laughter to reach his aim. He probably brought a little improvement in some conditions, but very often he failed to do so.

---

[13] *minor*, less important

WILLIAM MAKEPEACE THACKERAY studied and described the nobility instead of the poor. He followed in the footsteps of Fielding and Goldsmith. His best-known book, *Vanity Fair* (1847-8), describes the adventures of two girls of different sorts: Rebecca (Becky) Sharp, a clever, brave and poor girl without a conscience; and Amelia Sedley, the gentle daughter of a rich Londoner. The title of the novel comes from Bunyan's *Pilgrim's Progress. Pendennis* followed in 1848-50. *The Newcomes* (1853-5) is based on the life, love and marriage of Clive Newcome, the son of an honourable officer who loses all his money. *Henry Esmond* (1852) and *The Virginians* (1857-9) are historical novels.

An illustration drawn by Thackeray himself for his novel Vanity Fair

Thackeray gives a good picture of English society in the eighteenth century, and Steele, Addison and Swift are seen in his pages. Part of *The Virginians* deals with the American War of Independence.

Thackeray was not a romantic, and he did not produce his characters for the purpose of expressing violent feelings. He could describe strange qualities in human beings, and he could also show life's cruelties and people's weaknesses. He wrote as an educated man. Some of the characters in one novel are related to those in another. This gives an appearance of reality to the families concerned; yet many people find Thackeray hard to read. He is suspected of being very conscious of the importance of noble rank and good family, and this is looked on as a fault in the twentieth century.

We must now turn to Yorkshire where a girl, CHARLOTTE BRONTË, was brought up in poor surroundings. As a result of a stay in Brussels, she wrote *The Professor* (written in 1846 and published in 1857), which describes events in the life of a schoolmaster in that city. *Villette* (1853) uses the same material; it reflects the personal experiences of the writer when she was in Brussels; without beauty or money, the heroine becomes a teacher and wins respect by her fine character.

Her finest novel, *Jane Eyre* (1847), also describes the life of a poor and unbeautiful girl who is brought up by a cruel aunt and sent to a miserable school. After that she goes to teach the daughter of Mr Rochester at Thornfield Hall. Although she is not beautiful, Rochester falls in love with her; but when she discovers that his (mad) wife is still alive, she runs away. Later the Hall is burnt down and the mad wife is killed. In trying to save her, Rochester is blinded and loses all hope of happiness. On hearing of all this, Jane marries him and so is able to bring comfort into the remaining part of his life.

The book was very successful, although the heroine was neither beautiful nor rich. It is an honest description of strong feelings at a time when some feelings expressed in books were shallow. The power of the writing made it sell fast, and in a few months two more editions were printed. The dialogue[14] is more realistic[15] and less formal than in many novels of the period. Here are a few lines of

[14] *dialogue,* speech between two or more people.
[15] *realistic,* like real life.

dialogue between Jane Eyre and Rochester which come near the end of the book. (Jane's use of 'sir' might be explained by the fact that she had been Rochester's employee):

> 'Jane, will you marry me?'
> 'Yes, sir.'
> 'A poor blind man, whom you will have to lead about by the hand?'
> 'Yes, sir.'
> 'A crippled[A] man, twenty years older than you, whom you will have to wait on?'
> 'Yes, sir.'
> 'Truly, Jane?'
> 'Most truly, sir.'
> 'Oh! My darling![B] God bless you and reward you!'

[A] without a man's ordinary powers (i.e. blind)   [B] very dear one

Another, and less important, novel by the same writer is *Shirley* (1849), which is concerned with the wool industry, with riots, and with the Napoleonic wars.

Charlotte's sister, EMILY BRONTË, wrote one of the greatest of English novels, *Wuthering Heights* (1847). The passionate[16] Heathcliff falls in love with Catherine Earnshaw, but he hears her say that she could never marry such a low sort of creature, and so he leaves the house. Three years later, when he returns, he finds that Catherine has married Edgar Linton, a man of weak character. Heathcliff then begins a life of cruelty and revenge. Catherine dies, and Heathcliff marries Edgar's sister, and treats her very badly. The novel has been compared to Shakespeare's *King Lear*, chiefly because of its immense and uncontrollable passions. In the opinion of some critics, no woman could have written it; but others say that one man could not have written all the plays of Shakespeare!

Another woman novelist, known as GEORGE ELIOT, writes calmer books than this. Her real name was Mary Ann Evans. She lived abroad in Europe from 1854 to 1878, and married J. W. Cross a short time before her death.

[16] *passion*, powerful feelings; *passionate*, having such feelings.

Some of her early stories were collected under the title *Scenes from Clerical[17] Life* (1858) and her first novel was *Adam Bede* (1859), which was influenced by memories of her childhood. She showed at once that she could draw character and describe scenes with great skill, and that she had pity and humour. *The Mill on the Floss*[18] (1860) and *Silas Marner* (1861) followed, and then she wrote a historical novel about Florence, *Romola* (1863). *Middlemarch* appeared in 1871-2, and *Daniel Deronda* in 1876. To say which is her finest novel is not easy, but probably it is *Adam Bede* or *Middlemarch*. This latter novel is set in a provincial town where Dorothea Brooke, a girl of noble qualities, marries old Mr Casaubon; but the marriage is a failure. There is another plot, in which young Dr Lydgate marries the beautiful (but rather ordinary) Rosamond Vincy.

Elizabeth Cleghorn Stevenson became MRS GASKELL on her marriage. She is often considered as a one-novel writer because of the immense success of *Cranford* (1853), a delicate picture of life in a village. 'Cranford' is drawn from Knutsford in Cheshire, where Mrs Gaskell was brought up by an aunt. Social problems play a part; they do so in her other novels, but *Cranford* will live longest. The life of the village, where the ladies of good family are poor, is described with immense skill. (There are few gentlemen.) Miss Matty and Miss Deborah are among the chief characters. Imaginary robberies cause great fear in the village. The visit of a noble lady disturbs everyone. A cow gets into great trouble. At the end Miss Matty loses all her money, but friends help her; and her brother from India fortunately returns to England.

After her marriage to William Gaskell (1832), Mrs Gaskell lived in Manchester. Her other novels include *Mary Barton* (1848), which shows deep feeling for the poor people employed at this time in factories. *Ruth* (1853) is the sad story of a girl whose parents are dead. *North and South* (1854-5) is a study of the different lives led by English people, especially the poor in the north and the happier ones in the south. The plot centres round Margaret Hale, a gentle girl from the south, who goes north and meets the problems of angry crowds of poor workpeople. Mrs Gaskell also wrote a biography of Charlotte Brontë.

[17] *clerical*, of a priest.
[18] *Floss*, here a proper name.

CHARLES KINGSLEY, a historical novelist, set the scene of his novel *Hypatia* (1853) in Alexandria in the fifth century. Philammon, a young Christian, comes to the city from the desert and is much attracted by the teaching of the beautiful Hypatia. The picture of the city with all its crowded streets and troublesome problems is well drawn. When Hypatia is torn to pieces by an angry crowd, Philammon returns to the desert, a wiser man. The same writer's *Westward Ho!* (1855), *The Heroes* (1856), and *The Water Babies* (1863) are favourites among young people.

Practically the first English novelist to write detective[19] stories was WILLIAM WILKIE COLLINS, who occasionally worked with Dickens. His book *The Woman in White* (1860) is a complicated story about Walter Hartright, a drawing-master, who teaches a rich girl, Laura Fairlie. The woman dressed in white is Anne Catherick, who is shut up as mad. After many troubles and difficulties, Hartright marries Laura Fairlie. A famous character in the book is the fat, calm and evil Count Fosco, who is at last killed by a member of a secret society.

Collins's *The Moonstone* (1868) is another tale of mystery. A precious stone from India disappears, and the search for it brings out the character of Sergeant Cuff, one of the first detectives in English literature. Collins wrote several other novels, and also produced books with Dickens, such as *The Wreck of the Golden Mary* and *A Message from the Sea*.

CHARLES READE seems to have been a bad-tempered writer. He began by writing plays but turned one of them into a novel, *Peg Woffington* (1853). *It is Never too Late to Mend* (1856) was also a play at first. *Hard Cash* (1863) is one of the books that he wrote to try to improve social conditions: it shows the evils of madhouses at that time. His greatest work, the historical novel *The Cloister*[20] *and the Hearth*[21] (1861), is set in the fifteenth century. Gerard's adventures take him to prison, then away from his home in Holland, across Europe to Italy, and at last back to Holland. His son is supposed to be Erasmus, the great Dutch scholar and writer, who was born in

---

[19] *detective*, a man whose work is the tracking down of criminals; in detective novels the hero is usually employed to find, or prove the guilt of, a murderer.
[20] *cloister*, religious building.
[21] *hearth*, fireside.

1466. Reade wrote a number of other books. He was a hard worker, and a good teller of stories. He collected information as a regular duty, and kept a store of facts in great books in his London home.

ANTHONY TROLLOPE was a clerk who rose high in the service of the General Post Office, but by 1879 he had earned £70,000 by his books. Among the many novels that he wrote, *The Warden* (1855) is the first of those that are known as the Barsetshire novels. Barsetshire is the name given to the (imaginary) county[22] where the scenes are set. In these books he gave a picture of life in the country, at a distance from London, and especially the life of people connected with the Church. His other Barsetshire novels are *Barchester Towers* (1857), *Doctor Thorne* (1858), *Framley Parsonage* (1861), *The Small House at Allington* (1864) and *The Last Chronicle of Barset* (1867). 'Barchester' was probably drawn from either Winchester or Salisbury, or both. His characters are noticeably calm, almost ordinary, and give a picture of middle-class life in England.

Trollope wrote, as he himself said, like a machine, for three hours a day before breakfast, 5.30 a.m. to 8.30 a.m., forcing himself to write 1,000 words an hour. He always kept his watch in front of him, and because of this activity usually had one or two complete novels waiting for his publisher! This surely is very unusual!

The novels of GEORGE MEREDITH are difficult to read until one is accustomed to his tricks of style. *The Ordeal*[23] *of Richard Feverel* (1859) describes a boy's troubles when he is educated at home instead of going to school. Richard (who is of good family) falls in love with Lucy, a farmer's niece, and secretly marries her. His angry father separates the two, and then Richard goes to London, where he has many adventures, including another love affair. Later he is seriously wounded in a fight, and his wife Lucy dies of shock.

Meredith had to wait thirty years before he was widely read. *Diana of the Crossways* (1885) was popular, but the cause of this was partly artificial. The story was believed to be based on the true story of Caroline Norton, who was suspected at the time of selling an important state secret.

[22] *county*, local government division of Britain.
[23] *ordeal*, suffering.

Evan Harrington (1861) is the story of the son (Evan) of a splendid tailor. (Meredith's own father was a tailor at Portsmouth.) The story shows how the tailor's daughters do their best to escape from their connection with trade (always in those days a social disadvantage). One daughter marries a Portuguese nobleman. Evan himself is the centre of powerful influences which press him to marry into the nobility and forget tailoring; others try to make him return to his father's business.

In *The Egoist*[24] (1879), Meredith's best book, Sir Willoughby Patterne is a good picture of a man very pleased with himself; and Clara Middleton is Meredith's most attractive heroine. One or two other characters in the book are half-pictures of men alive at the time. Meredith's difficult and musical style is especially noticeable in some of the descriptions of nature.

It is not often that a man of one nation learns the language of another and then writes fine novels in it; yet that is what JOSEPH CONRAD did. His original name was Teodor Josef Konrad Korzeniowsky. He was born and brought up in Poland and knew little or nothing of England when he first visited it in 1878; yet by 1884 he had qualified as a captain of British ships, and in 1895 he produced his first novel in English, *Almayer's Folly*. In his own fine style he wrote better than many Englishmen, though occasionally a sentence or a group of sentences is too complicated to be immediately clear. He had much to write about because he had travelled widely and seen a great deal of the world. One of his guiding beliefs was that a man must always be faithful to his friends, his fellows and his employers. If there is no faithfulness between man and man, ruin is certain to follow. Conrad's heroes, rather like Shakespeare's, have within themselves weaknesses which destroy them if they can.

Some readers notice Conrad's language difficulties in the early novels, such as *Almayer's Folly* (1895) and *An Outcast*[25] *of the Islands* (1896). *Lord Jim* (1900), one of his greatest novels, tells the story of an Englishman who leaves a ship that seems to be sinking and so loses his honour, but dies an honourable death later. *Youth, Heart of Darkness*, and *Typhoon*[26] are shorter stories, but very fine work.

---

[24] *egoist*, one who thinks only of himself.
[25] *outcast*, a man not accepted by his fellow-men.
[26] *typhoon*, storm.

The last of these describes a ship in a violent storm; the lonely courage of Captain MacWhirr is well brought out and it appears even finer because he is a man whose wife scorns him and whose men do not understand him. Conrad's powers of description are fully used in the picture of the machinery in the engine-room during the height of the storm.

The Secret Agent (1907) and *Under Western Eyes* (1911) are among the good novels of later dates. Conrad's prose is richer than that of many English writers, and his art is European rather than English.

ROBERT LOUIS STEVENSON studied engineering and the law before he wrote books. His weak lungs drove him to travel in search of health and *Inland Voyage* (1878) and *Travels with a Donkey* (1879) are descriptions of journeys that he made. Later he wrote essays, short stories and novels. His essays include *Virginibus Puerisque* [= For girls and boys] (1881) and *Familiar Studies of Men and Books* (1882). *Treasure Island* (1883) is an adventure story which is still popular, and *The New Arabian Nights* (1882) is a book of stories which almost make us believe the impossible. *Kidnapped* (1886), a story of adventure in Scotland, still attracts readers, and so do *The Black Arrow* (1888) and *The Master of Ballantrae* (1889). Stevenson's best plot is perhaps that of *The Strange Case of Dr Jekyll and Mr Hyde;* in this exciting novel the reader follows the struggle between two forms of the same man – the good Dr Jekyll and the evil Mr Hyde.

ANTHONY HOPE was the pen-name of Anthony Hope Hawkins. He left us two very popular novels of adventure in an imaginary country, 'Ruritania'. These are *The Prisoner of Zenda* (1894) and *Rupert of Hentzau* (1898), which is a continuation and includes the same characters. The reason for the continuing popularity of these books is probably to be found in the powerful love interest, the attraction of the chief characters, and the clear descriptions of astonishing events. Another book by the same writer, *The Dolly Dialogues* (1894), contains amusing conversations without much story.

OSCAR WILDE wrote a few works of fiction, the most important being *The Picture of Dorian Gray* (1891), a novel which gave the public of the time a severe shock. Wilde's plays are discussed in another chapter.

In the novels of THOMAS HARDY nature plays an important part; indeed Nature is herself a character. Hardy's scenes are set in 'Wessex' (the county of Dorset) among trees, farms, fields, and low hills. Hardy believed that the past has built up a mass of conditions which remain to influence people's lives; and he also thought that blind chance has a very important effect. The best way of life is therefore to accept calmly the blows of fate. His novels, spread over the years 1870-96, are mostly pictures of human beings struggling against fate or chance.

Far From The Madding[27] *Crowd* (1874) is the story of patient love on one side, and selfish passion on the other. Gabriel Oak, a shepherd, loves Bathsheba Everdene with a true heart and serves her faithfully for many years; but Sergeant Try, an attractive but cruel soldier, marries her and treats her badly. He is murdered by an angry farmer, and after many troubles Bathsheba marries Oak. Another sad story of love affairs and jealousy is *The Return of the Native* (1878).

In *The Mayor*[28] *of Casterbridge* (1886) Michael Henchard, while he is drunk, sells his wife and children for a few pounds. Later, realising what he has done, he decides not to touch strong drink again for twenty years. He works hard, becomes rich, and is made Mayor of Casterbridge. After eighteen years his wife returns, but that is not the end of their troubles. Henchard is ruined, and starts drinking again. He dies miserably.

Tess of the D'Urbervilles (1891) is a tale of a poor girl, Tess Durbeyfield, whose misfortunes are so great that in the end she murders a man and is hanged. Her poor father's life is upset when he learns that he is descended from an ancient family, the D'Urbervilles. Tess is wrongfully treated by Alec D'Urberville, whose family do not have a clear right to their name. Misfortune follows Tess through her life and she dies only when fate has lost interest in her.

Hardy's last novel, *Jude the Obscure*[29] (1896), is extremely miserable, and it may be true that he turned to poetry to escape from such terrible products of his imagination. Jude is a poor stone-worker

---

[27] *madding*, maddening. (Hardy's title is part of a line from Gray's Elegy Written in a Country Churchyard – see page 76).

[28] *mayor*, chairman of a town council.

[29] *obscure*, unknown.

who wants to educate himself; but though he has a fine spirit, he has little control of his passions, and he does not learn much. Fate is against him. His marriage is a failure, and he falls in love with a clever teacher. Sorrow follows their life together; their children die; then Jude begins to drink and dies unhappily.

Hardy wrote a few novels of a different kind. His novels of romance include *A Pair of Blue Eyes* (1873) and *The Trumpet Major* (1880). His first published novel, *Desperate Remedies* (1871) is again of a different sort. It depends for its effect on surprise and mystery.

An illustration from Thomas Hardy's Tess of the D'Urbervilles.

Charles Darwin's scientific writing had an important influence on nineteenth-century thought

Chapter Twelve

Other nineteenth-century prose

In addition to the novels which the century produced, a large amount of good prose set forth the ideas of the time. CHARLES LAMB is well known for his *Essays of Elia* (1823 and 1833), essays on various light subjects written in an attractive style. With his sister, Mary Lamb, he also wrote his *Tales from Shakespeare* (1807). In the next year he produced his *Specimens*[1] *of English Dramatic Poets*. Lamb also wrote a few poems; one of the best of them is *The Old Familiar Faces* (1798): 'All, all are gone, the old familiar faces'.

WILLIAM HAZLITT, another essayist of the time, was a quarrelsome man. His most important work is probably his literary criticism: *Characters of Shakespeare's Plays* (1817-8), *Lectures on the English Poets* (1818-9), *English Comic Writers* (1819), and so on. The gentle ways of Charles Lamb were charming, but Hazlitt was less likeable. He was a man in public affairs, but Lamb was a private person. Hazlitt's standard of dramatic criticism was high, but his bad temper and his political ideas led him into violent language and fits of anger which occasionally spoilt his judgment.

THOMAS DE QUINCEY was an even more unpleasant person than Hazlitt, but his work cannot be dismissed as valueless. He first became famous through his *Confessions of an English Opium*[2] *Eater* (1822). He describes how he was first driven to the taking of opium

---

[1] *specimen*, example.
[2] *opium*, a substance which has an effect on the brain; taken either as smoke or as medicine it is dangerously habit-forming.

by violent toothache and attacks of anxiety. He had bad dreams and other unpleasant effects from the opium for eight years. He conquered the habit by great efforts which caused more suffering. His prose is fine when it is at its best, plain when he describes something plain, and much ornamented when, for example, he describes an opium dream. His *Reminiscences*[3] *of the English Lake Poets* (1834) contain some good chapters on Wordsworth and Coleridge. Other essays were on various subjects. One of them was *On Murder Considered as One of the Fine Arts.*

THOMAS CARLYLE was another writer of the time who was unattractive as a man, cold, self-centred, and unwilling to accept anyone as his better. One of his early works was a translation of part of Goethe's *Wilhelm Meister* (1824). He wrote articles in various papers, but his *Sartor Resartus* [=The Tailor Repaired] was not published as a book in Britain until 1838, though it had appeared in a paper four or five years before that, and in America two years before. The first part of it declares that all human arrangements are like clothes, and do not last long. The second part is an autobiography[4] of Carlyle himself. He says that at one time he saw the heaven and earth as the open jaws of a great creature ready to eat him; but he shook off his fear when he asked himself, 'What *art* thou afraid of?'

Carlyle's style was forceful, even violent. His guiding aims in life were truth, work and courage. His famous *History of the French Revolution* (1837) is a picture of passion and flame, for which his style is suitable. Other important works by Carlyle include *Heroes and Hero-Worship* (Carlyle did not believe in equality among men, but in the rule of the strong). He also wrote a *History of Frederick the Great* (1858-65). It is an interesting book, but all the work that he spent on it ought to have produced something better.

Another historian, THOMAS BABINGTON MACAULAY, had one of the world's most astonishing memories. When he was still a boy, he could say the whole of *Paradise Lost* from beginning to end. The first article that he wrote was on Milton (1825). His splendid store of knowledge was regularly increased by reading. He studied law,

---

[3] *reminiscence*, a thing remembered, such as an event in one's childhood.
[4] *autobiography*, one person's life story written by himself; *autobiographical*, referring to one's own life.

entered Parliament (1830), went to India, and then returned to English politics. In verse his *Lays of Ancient Rome* were an attempt in English to write the lost ballads of Rome. One of them is on the subject of how Horatius defended a bridge against the Tuscans. His verse is not great, but it is strong and clear. Elizabeth Barrett said that he had a metallic soul.

Macaulay's fame rests on his historical, and also slightly on his critical, works. His prose style is usually fine and strong; sometimes numbers of short sentences follow each other like sharp explosions; in other places the prose style has a steady beat like great waves rolling in from the ocean – notice the balance produced by three statements in the same form, followed by the point to be made, in these words from an essay on Boswell's Life of Johnson:

> The Life of Johnson is assuredly[A] a great, a very great work. Homer is not more decidedly the first of heroic poets, Shakespeare is not more decidedly the first of dramatists, Demosthenes is not more decidedly the first of orators, than Boswell is the first of biographers.
>
> [A] certainly

Macaulay's famous *History of England* (1848, 1855) was immediately popular, but his opinions are often narrow-minded and he has been accused of reaching wrong conclusions. Yet on facts we can usually depend on Macaulay's splendid memory. Both he and Carlyle increased the value of their histories by visiting the scenes of events, and so being able to describe them more clearly.

CHARLES ROBERT DARWIN in *A Naturalist's Voyage Round the World* (1839), gave a description of his journey in the ship 'Beagle'. This and other early writings gave Darwin a high position among scientists. *The Origin of Species*[5] (1859) was the result of 20 years of study and enquiries among gardeners and farmers. He became quite sure that plants and animals which suited their surroundings were more likely to live than those which did not. He began to write down his ideas in 1842. In 1858 ALFRED RUSSEL WALLACE, who was then in the islands of south-east Asia suddenly thought of the idea

[5] *species*, kind (of living thing – scientists divide a *genus* of plants or animals of the same general kind into various *species* of particular kinds).

Afternoon tea in British India in the 1880s

of natural selection,[6] wrote an essay on it, and sent it to Darwin. Thus two great men had the same idea at the same time. An outline of Darwin's book, and Wallace's essay on the same subject, were published in 1858.

The book shows a wide and calm gift of suggestion. It is well balanced, and the arguments are neither too long nor too short. The book itself is a fine example of selection of material. Its publication was followed by a storm of criticism on one side, and a hearty welcome on the other; but when passions had calmed down, its qualities and theories were discussed in a better spirit.

Darwin's most important book after *The Origin of Species* is *The Descent of Man* (1871), which applies the ideas of the earlier book to the human race. Wallace did not agree with Darwin in this; he believed that natural selection alone could not have produced the human brain.

[6] *selection*, choosing; *natural selection*, is the way in which nature chooses the form of plant or animal most suitable for a purpose.

The ugliness of the industrial world at this time brought anger into the heart of JOHN RUSKIN, who was a student of art. He praised some of the new painters such as Turner in *Modern Painters* (1843-60). He defended Gothic architecture in *The Seven Lamps of Architecture* (1849). The seven lamps are Sacrifice, Truth, Power (the use of shadow), Beauty, Life, Memory and Obedience. He continued this idea in *The Stones of Venice* (1851-3). The beauty that he loved and aimed at is to be found in his own prose style, much ornamented but based on the language of the Bible. His later books were on economics[7] and education, but he always had before him the aim of a beautiful world.

WALTER PATER studied Ruskin's works but did not arrive at the same conclusions.[8] For Pater, art of all kinds should aim at beauty for no social or moral reason – just because the search for beauty is a satisfying activity in itself. He developed this idea in clear and beautiful prose in essays, in a longer work, *Conclusion to Studies in the History of the Renaissance*[9] (1873), and in a novel set in ancient Rome, *Marius the Epicurean* (1885).

At about this time a university teacher of mathematics[10] at Oxford was Charles Lutwidge Dodgson, who wrote under the pen-name, LEWIS CARROLL. He is remembered more for his two books for children than for his excellent mathematics. *Alice's Adventures in Wonderland* (1865) was written for a young girl, Alice, but is read now by grown-ups too, because the nonsense in it is not only delightful but strangely reasonable. The book has remained popular ever since its publication. Here is a verse from one of the poems:

'You are old, Father William,' the young man said,
　'And your hair has become very white;
And yet you incessantly[A] stand on your head.
　Do you think, at your age, it is right?'

[A] often

---

[7] *economics*, the science of the production and use of wealth.

[8] *conclusion*, the opinion reached after considering all the arguments.

[9] *the Renaissance*, the great growth of interest in art and literature in the fourteenth to sixteenth centuries in Europe following the 'Dark Ages' and resulting from a rediscovery of the Greek and Roman classics and art.

[10] *mathematics*, the science of number, space and quantity.

A later book, *Through the Looking-Glass* (1872), continues the strange adventures of Alice, and also contains some absolute nonsense:

> 'Twas brillig and the slithy toves
>   Did gyre and gimble in the wabe;
> All mimsy were the borogoves
>   And the mome raths outgrabe.

This splendid poem has no meaning at all, and yet we feel that there must be strange creatures in the wabe, whatever that is. The great scientist, SIR ARTHUR STANLEY EDDINGTON, said later in *The Nature of the Physical World* (1928) that the universe is like the place in Carroll's poem. We know that something is doing something somewhere, but we do not understand exactly what is happening.

We have seen that names from Shakespeare's plays, Bunyan's *Pilgrim's Progress* and Dickens's novels have become household words in English. Carroll's two Alice books are another source of this kind, and modern writers will refer, without considering any explanation necessary, to the Duchess, the Cheshire Cat, the Mad Hatter, Tweedledum and Tweedledee, the Red Queen, the White Knight, and many another of the curious creatures, playing-card characters and unusual chessmen[11] of this back-to-front world.

MATTHEW ARNOLD, already mentioned in the chapter on poetry,

An illustration to
Alice in Wonderland
by J. Tenniel

---

[11] *chess*, a game played on a board between two players with 16 *chessmen* each, the aim being to trap the other player's king.

wrote several important books of criticism in prose. He wanted English writers to remember the eighteenth century and the classics. *On Translating Homer* (1861), and *Essays in Criticism* (1865, 1888) point this way. He also criticised English social and political life in *Culture and Anarchy*[12] (1869).

An attack on society came from another direction. Victorian society stood as firm as a rock in its belief in its own rightness until SAMUEL BUTLER attacked it with satire. He was at first a sheep farmer in New Zealand and made enough money there to return to England and live in moderate comfort. His *Erewhon* (1872) is a satire on English customs. The title is the name of an imaginary country [=Nowhere] cut off from the world by high mountains. In spite of these, a traveller reaches the place. It is a strange country. Its people are beautiful but their ideas are different from those of Europe. If a man is poor in Erewhon, he is a criminal. If he is sick, he is a criminal. If he is ugly, he is a criminal. But if he does something that we consider to be a crime, he is sent to hospital, not to prison. There he is cured of his crimes by doctors who are called Straighteners. Many other ideas are back to front. The musical banks are like churches. They have a special sort of money which is, in fact, useless. There are Colleges of Unreason. Machines are not allowed; they have all been destroyed because the rulers think them dangerous. They might rule the country themselves if they were allowed to develop. This unusual book was followed by another, *Erewhon Revisited* (1901).

The Way of All Flesh (1903), a novel published after his death, was Butler's autobiographical study of parents and children, and the fortunes of the Pontifex family. It is, on the whole, a dark book, with a few brighter parts.

Butler did not agree at all with Darwin and argued against him in *Life and Habit* (1877) and other books. In these he said that habits and qualities are handed down from father to son. He also developed an interest in ancient Greek, and translated Homer's *Iliad* and *Odyssey*. Like the Greeks, he believed that everything must be in moderation, that we must have 'nothing too much'. He tried to prove that the *Odyssey* was written by a woman.

[1,2] *anarchy*, having no order or rules – and so, in Arnold's title, the opposite of *culture*, improvement by education.

This statue of the Irish novelist James Joyce stands over his grave in Zurich, Switzerland

Chapter Thirteen

Twentieth-century novels and other prose

The English novels of the nineteenth century were written at a time of great confidence in British society, culture and political organization (affecting not only Britain, but the Empire overseas), and although different novelists present groups of characters from different levels of society and explore different themes, there is a sense of confidence in the basic structure of society, and the place of people in it, that underlies their work. The writers of the twentieth century could not share this confidence; the changes in beliefs and political ideas were influenced strongly by the events of the First World War and by the events across the world that led to the disappearance of the British Empire, but began even earlier.

This change can be seen by comparing two writers working close to each other in time, but with a great distance between them in terms of beliefs and ideas. RUDYARD KIPLING was born in India and spent much of his adult life there, at a time when the power and influence of the British Empire was at its height. The poems and short stories for which he is best known deal with India itself, its wild animals, and the British army and navy. His best-known books are *The Jungle*[1] *Book* (1894), which describes how the boy Mowgli is brought up in the jungle by wild animals who have human personalities, and *Kim* (1901), the story of a boy in India who grows up to do service to the British Empire by capturing some important secret papers. Kipling writes with certainty that the beliefs and values of his stories are accepted and shared completely by his readers.

[1] *jungle*, a thick forest in a hot country.

E.M. FORSTER, working at very much the same time (his first novel, *Where Angels Fear to Tread*, was published in 1905), takes a completely different view of the values which formed and governed British society at that time and on which the British Empire was based. *Howard's End* (1910) shows the completely different beliefs of two families, the Wilcoxes (who are good at making money and are concerned only with everyday things that they can see and touch) and the two Schlegel sisters (who are concerned with deeper, more spiritual and cultural values). The two families struggle for the house named in the title, which stands for England itself. Forster's theme is how to connect the everyday 'outer' life of the Wilcoxes with the inner life of the heart and spirit represented by the Schlegels: 'Only connect the prose and the passion, and both will be exalted[2], and human love will be seen at its height.'

Like Kipling, Forster spent some time in India, but his view of the country, seen in *A Passage to India* (1924), is very different. He shows most of the English who governed India at that time as the same sort of people as the Wilcoxes in *Howard's End*, busy with traditional[3] ways of behaving and the appearance of things and people, and unable to see the inner truth of events. The story concerns Adela, an Englishwoman who has gone to India to marry an English official there; she makes friends with some Indians, but is led to believe that one of them attacks her sexually on a visit to some caves. When she accuses him (and later takes back the accusation) she causes the separation in beliefs, behaviour and attitudes of the English from the Indians to become even stronger and more violent. Forster's theme, here as well, is the importance of bringing together opposites (in societies, different people and within one character) to make a complete and healthy whole. Forster also points out that the people who are failures in terms of money and worldly importance may in fact be successful: 'There are many types of failure, some of which succeed.'

Although Forster was presenting new ideas about people and society, the form of the novel that he used followed the traditional pattern. The traditional form was also used by ARNOLD BENNETT, but with greater realism in the presentation of the details of the characters' lives. Many of his novels were set in 'the Five Towns', the area in the

[2] *exalted*, made higher and greater.
[3] *traditional*, following usual beliefs and practice.

At work in the Potteries at the turn of the century

centre of England also known as the Potteries, where pots, cups, saucers etc. have been made for over two hundred years. *The Old Wives' Tale* (1908) contrasts the lives of two sisters from this part of England. One runs away with a man who later leaves her in Paris with no friends or money, and who has to make a life there for herself with no one to help her; the other sister stays at home, marries a man who works in her father's shop, and lives the settled, dull life expected of her without wishing for anything more. In his group of novels about the Five Towns (*Clayhanger*, 1910; *Hilda Lessways*, 1911; *These Twain*, 1916), Bennett follows the lives of the same group of characters, with the industrial background of the area playing an important part. He also wrote *Riceyman Steps* (1923), about the life and death of a London bookseller whose main concern in life is to save money. His novels give a picture of life that is harder and duller than that given by most earlier writers.

H. G. WELLS also often took characters from a lower social level, but many of his characters are given a chance of happiness. *Kipps* (1905) and *The History of Mr Polly* (1910) both deal with men working in shops who find that the things they thought would change their lives (money in the first case, running away in the second) do not bring them what they hoped for, but at the end of the novels they know better what they need to be happy. Wells also used modern scientific advances in his novels, in a new way: *The Time Machine* (1895) is about a machine that can travel through time instead of through space; *The War of the Worlds*

(1898) describes an attack on this world by men from Mars, who can conquer everything but man's diseases; *The First Men on the Moon* (1901) shows men flying to the moon about seventy years before this actually happened. He also wrote *Ann Veronica* (1909) about a girl who wants to choose for herself what to do in life, which in many ways also looks ahead to the women's movement much later this century.

SOMERSET MAUGHAM's first novel, *Lisa of Lambeth* (1897) gave a realistic picture of slum[4] life, and the novel based on his own life, *Of Human Bondage*[5] (1915) showed the hardship and difficulties of his own early life. But *The Moon and Sixpence* (1919), which used the life-story of the French artist Gauguin (who left his ordinary life in France and went to live and paint on an island in the South Seas) presents a new figure as hero, the artist who is fighting against conventional society. *Cakes and Ale* (1930) is a satire on the English social and literary life of the first part of the century, and has a warmth not found in all his work. He is perhaps best known for his short stories: for example, the collection published in 1928 under the title *Ashenden*. Ashenden is a spy, another figure who has become very popular as a hero in English fiction during this century, and the character who tells the story became particularly associated with Maugham himself in the minds of the public. He is shown as a man who has travelled widely and has a great knowledge of people and places as well as expensive food and drink. Maugham is a sharp observer of people, and is amused by them, but does not want to get closely involved with them. He wants to tell good stories rather than to explore character deeply, and the stories often have a bitter or unexpected ending.

D. H. LAWRENCE's view of the writer's purpose was very different: he felt it was the novelist's job to show how an individual's view of his own personality was often affected by conventions of language, family and religion, and to show how people and their relationships with each other were always changing and moving. He took the form of the traditional novel and made it wider and deeper. Much of *Sons and Lovers* (1913) is taken from his own early life: his hero, Paul Morel, grows up near Nottingham in the English Midlands as Lawrence did, and also wants to be a creative artist. The centre of the novel is the relationship between Paul and his mother: he loves her and needs her

---

[4] *slum*, a city area with poor and dirty living conditions.
[5] *bondage*, the condition of being a slave.

Glenda Jackson and Jennie Linden in the film of Women in Love

to help him make sense of the world around him, but in order to become an independent man and a true artist he has to make his own decisions about his life and work, and has to struggle to become free from her influence. Like Forster's characters, Paul Morel needs to put the outer and inner world together in a true relation. Lawrence shows how the daily life of his characters influences them (Paul's father is affected by his life as a miner, and Miriam, one of the women Paul loves, is influenced by her life on the farm) but he is also concerned to express the inner qualities of human nature. This is often done through a description of nature – when Miriam watches a sunset with Paul, Lawrence's description gives the story of their relationship:

> She went to the fence and sat there, watching the gold clouds fall to pieces, and go in immense, rose-coloured ruin towards the darkness. Gold flamed to scarlet[A], like pain in the intense[B] brightness. Then the scarlet sank to rose, and rose to crimson[C], and quickly the passion went out of the sky. All the world was dark grey.
> [A] bright red   [B] very strong   [C] deep red

The Rainbow[6] (finished in 1915) tells the story of a family through three couples of different ages. The first couple, Lydia and Tom, have a deep

    [6] *rainbow*, an arch of different colours that sometimes appears in the sky after rain.

and loving understanding of each other and can also communicate with the outside world; the second couple (Lydia's daughter Anna and Tom's nephew Will) have physical passion for each other, but, in Lawrence's words, 'their souls remain separate'. The third couple (Anna and Will's daughter Ursula and her lover Anton) use language as a wall to keep them apart at the deepest level, and each tries to force their own wishes on the other. Lawrence says of the first couple, 'There was an inner reality, a logic[7] of the soul, which connected her with him', but the other couples have lost their reality and their inner lives are poorer as a result.

Women in Love (finished in 1916) shows two couples – the women are sisters, the men are connected by close friendship – trying to understand the true meaning of love and to work towards a real closeness of souls. As in *The Rainbow*, relationships between men and women are seen growing and changing through time, and there is also a powerful sense of the presence of nature and how small man is in comparison:

> Whatever the mystery which has brought forth[A] man and the universe, it is a non-human mystery, it has its own great ends, man is not the criterion.[B]
>
> [A] produced   [B] standard by which something is judged

JAMES JOYCE was born and educated in Ireland and spent most of his adult life in Europe, mainly in France, Italy and Switzerland. His first short stories, published as *Dubliners*[8] (1914), are realistic on the surface but also carry a deeper meaning; *The Dead*, in which a husband is shocked out of his self-satisfaction by discovering his wife's love for a dead man she knew many years before, is the most notable. *A Portrait*[9] *of the Artist as a Young Man* (1916) presents Joyce himself as a young man in the character of his hero, Stephen Dedalus, who is formed by the powerful forces of Irish national, political and religious feelings, and shows how he gradually frees himself from the influence of these forces to follow his own nature and his own fate.

Stephen Dedalus also appears as a character in *Ulysses* (1922), a book which is regarded as one of the most important novels in English

---

[7] *logic*, reason.
[8] *Dubliners*, people from Dublin, the capital of Ireland.
[9] *portrait*, picture.

of the century. In *Ulysses*, Joyce created a completely new style of writing which allows the reader to move inside the minds of the characters, and presents their thoughts and feelings in a continuous stream, breaking all the usual rules of description, speech and punctuation. This style is known as 'interior[10] monologue[11]' or 'stream of consciousness', and it has had a powerful influence on the work of many other writers.

Ulysses has no real plot[12], but follows the three main characters – Stephen, Leopold Bloom and his wife Molly – through a day in Dublin. The characters and parts of the novel are connected with and reflect characters and events from ancient Greek stories, as the title suggests. The novel is funny, touching and often satirical; some events are clearly fanciful, while other parts of the book are completely realistic. Joyce is again concerned with the artist and the nature of the act of artistic creation, and also with the relationship between mind and body, especially when he is attempting to show all the half-formed thoughts that go through the characters' minds. At the end of the novel, Molly is lying in bed; among many thoughts that go through her mind, she is planning a musical evening:

> what shall I wear shall I wear a white rose those cakes in Liptons I love the smell of a rich big shop at $7\frac{1}{2}$d[A] a pound or the other ones with the cherries[B] in them of course a nice plant for the middle of the table I love flowers Id love to have the whole place swimming in roses God of heaven theres nothing like nature the wild mountains then the sea and the waves rushing then the beautiful country with fields of all kinds of things and all the fine cattle[C] going about that would do your heart good to see rivers and lakes and flowers . . .
>
> [A] pence   [B] small red fruit   [C] cows

Finnegan's Wake[13] (1939) takes one step further the new type of language which Joyce was starting to create in *Ulysses*; here, not only the

[10] *interior*, inside.
[11] *monologue*, something spoken by one person.
[12] *plot*, the story of a book, play, film, etc.
[13] *wake*, a meeting to watch over a dead person on the night before the burial.

Portrait of Virginia Woolf by Vanessa Bell

sentences are mixed up but the forms of the words themselves. Again, Joyce uses references to ancient stories to express the themes of the nature of creation (of the artist and of God) and the humour and tragedy of human life; but the difficulty of the language, in which Joyce is forcing as many associations as possible into each word, gives many readers great problems of understanding.

VIRGINIA WOOLF was also attempting to explore the consciousness of her characters, but she was not attempting to deal with so many types of people and situations as James Joyce was. *Mrs Dalloway* (1925) gives a description of one day in June 1923 as it was experienced by Mrs Dalloway and other characters. *To the Lighthouse* (1927) begins by presenting a family on holiday in Scotland in September 1910. The youngest son, James Ramsay, wants very much to go by boat to the lighthouse but is prevented by his father, and the novel ends with the same family in the same house ten years later; James at last goes to the lighthouse, but this time he hates his father for making him go as much as he earlier hated him for preventing it. The novel presents two kinds of truth – Mr Ramsay's, which is the truth of facts that can be proved, and Mrs Ramsay's, which is an attempt to find the truth that lies below the facts.

Orlando (1928) presents a main character who begins as a man in the sixteenth century and ends as a woman in 1928, still only thirty-six years old. Although, as this suggests, the surface of the story is fanciful and often amusing, there is also a serious point to be made in that Orlando only understands the truth of things when he/she stops separating the different parts of his/her character. *The Waves* (1931) takes six characters at different points of their lives and shows how each is affected by the death of a person they all knew well. Virginia Woolf also wrote many critical studies, on literature and other subjects.

GRAHAM GREENE divides his many books into two groups: serious novels and entertainments. In his serious novels the characters who are failures – in comparison with what they wanted and hoped to do – are seen as being nearer God than those who are more successful in worldly ways. *Brighton Rock* (1938) has at its centre an evil man who thinks he can conquer everything and everyone who stands in his way. He is outside the laws of man, but for Greene only God's law is strong enough to reach him: his soul can after all be saved because he did love, once. *The Power and the Glory* (1940), one of Green's strongest novels, tells the story of a priest in South America who is in danger from the forces of the state and has the choice of saving his soul (by continuing to act as a priest) or his body (either by escaping or by breaking the promises he made when he became a priest). He knows very well the weakness of his own nature and this, to Greene, makes him more able to rise to spiritual greatness than a man who had not done so much wrong.

JOYCE CARY's best-known novel remains *The Horse's Mouth* (1944), which shows great cleverness in his use of language to give this picture of an artist who lives for his art, but in its belief that art can conquer the rest of the world it has a hope for the future that is very different from most of the other novels being written at this time.

Certainly the novels of WILLIAM GOLDING do not share this hope. His first novel, and still his best known, is *Lord of the Flies* (1954), which describes how a group of English schoolboys are wrecked on a desert island, and how the effects of civilization break down and they return to their essential animal nature – which is, for Golding, the essential nature of all human beings. They are divided into two groups – those who guard the fire (the dreamers and poets) and those who hunt for food (the men of action) – and the novel shows how the two groups

Iris Murdoch

cannot work together for the good of them all, but attack and try to destroy each other with frightening violence. His later novels also consider absolute values of good and evil and the essential nature of man, *Pincher Martin* (1956) by showing the struggle of a shipwrecked sailor to stay alive until he is found, and *The Spire* (1964) showing a man's attempt to build a great church from a feeling of pride as well as a wish to praise God.

IRIS MURDOCH's novel *The Bell* (1958) takes a similar subject – in this case, the attempt of a group of people leading a religious life to set up a bell – but the world she creates is very different from Golding's. Hers is a mixture of the serious and the fanciful, and her characters fall into two general groups: those who have a very strong aim in life and cannot really notice anything else, and those whose life has not yet settled into a fixed pattern and are still willing to make changes. *A Severed[14] Head* (1961) is a sharp comedy that describes different ideas and patterns of love; a mixture of humour and sadness is presented with great skill in the use of language. Some of her later novels are an interesting second consideration of a theme she had used earlier. For example, her first novel *Under the Net* (1954) and *The Black Prince* (1973) both show the struggle between the pressure to tell the truth on

[14] *severed*, cut off.

one hand and the need for imagination to make life bearable on the other, and she also shows that the act of describing something in language always changes the way in which people think about it.

The many different novels of ANTHONY BURGESS cover a very wide area. He admires the work of James Joyce, and like him enjoys exploring the possibilities of language. His early novels show other influences also: his three novels set in Malaya (*The Malayan Trilogy*, 1956–59) owe a lot to E. M. Forster's *A Passage to India* in the picture they give of a British schoolmaster surrounded by a large group of very different characters of different races, personalities, beliefs and interests. Burgess's best-known book is probably *A Clockwork[15] Orange* (1962), a picture of the future in which Alex, the leader of a group of young men, does many evil things because he consciously chooses to do so. We see his cruelty and his pleasure in causing pain and unhappiness, and we see the suffering of the people he hurts; but Burgess is making the moral point that the most important thing is that Alex can choose whether he does good or evil. Later, Alex is caught and treated by doctors with electric shocks to 'cure' him of wanting to cause pain in others, but to Burgess man's 'good' actions are worth nothing if he does them because he has to and not because he wants to. The story is told by Alex in a type of language invented by Burgess, which is based on English but includes many words from other languages, particularly Russian.

Burgess's other novels are entertaining stories and also, like *A Clockwork Orange*, make a moral point. *The Wanting Seed* (1962), for example, which is also set in the England of the future, shows with great satirical energy how too many people living in a small country lead to a government decision to take human life, while *Tremor[16] of Intent* (1966), in the line of spy novels by Conrad and Graham Greene, shows the problem of morality of a secret agent.

ANGUS WILSON's novels in many ways use the traditional form of the novel developed by nineteenth-century writers like Dickens (on whom Wilson has also written) to give a picture of twentieth-century life and to consider the new problems it raises. His early collections of short stories (*The Wrong Set*, 1949; *Such Darling Dodos[17]*, 1950) are often satirical and make a moral judgement on the patterns of life he sees

[15] *clockwork*, worked by machinery.
[16] *tremor*, a shaking movement.
[17] *dodo*, a large bird that no longer exists.

around him, although this is not always expressed directly. *Anglo-Saxon Attitudes* (1956) covers much more ground through its story of a historian who is forced by events to tell the truth, both about a historical discovery and about himself; there is irony in the fact that at the end of the novel his professional life as a historian is becoming successful, but all his personal relationships have failed. *The Middle Age of Mrs Eliot* (1958) gives a picture of a woman whose husband has just died. She gradually becomes able to experience deep feelings again, and she refuses the protected and comfortable life her family offers to live alone and come to know the world around her, so that, as she says, 'the modern world won't be able to take me by surprise again.'

Of his later novels, *No Laughing Matter* (1967) shows how a family's confidence in their way of life breaks into pieces under the pressures of the modern world. *As If By Magic* (1973) has two main characters, a young girl student and a middle-aged scientist, who meet unexpectedly in India. The girl, Alexandra, in some ways the more interesting character, realizes at the end of the novel that one cannot escape the past and future, and that there is no magic to solve human problems; she is determined to find a moral position between those who give orders and those who want to be given them.

Although Wilson's novels present many different types of character, most are drawn from the same social group, the middle class. At the same time that writers in the theatre and cinema were exploring the worlds of characters from much lower social levels in a realistic way, many novelists were attempting the same thing, and it is interesting that the two best-known novels by ALAN SILLITOE have been made into films. *Saturday Night and Sunday Morning* (1958) shows a young man from the working class in a town in the English Midlands who is determined to do what he wants to in life and not what the rules of the society in which he lives say is the right thing to do. *The Loneliness of the Long-Distance Runner* (1959) shows how one of the boys in a boys' prison refuses to do what the governor of the prison wants him to do; by losing a race which the governor wants him to win, he keeps his pride in himself and his own sense of freedom.

The novels of KINGSLEY AMIS have greater comedy and less moral concern. The best known, *Lucky Jim* (1954) shows the attempts of a young university teacher to break the rules of his social class and connect with the working class and unusual characters outside any social group, who experience a different sort of life from the one he knows and who, in his opinion, have stronger and deeper feelings than the people around him.

EVELYN WAUGH is probably the greatest English comic novelist of the century. His most characteristic novels are very satirical, with comically unsympathetic characters who are often cruelly described, and stories that are amusing and often completely impossible to believe. *Decline and Fall* (1928), his first novel, sets the pattern through its story of a young man's innocence and the world's dishonesty. Waugh enjoys the comic effects of confusion, physical as well as moral; his characters can be persuaded to do anything and to accept any idea, however laughable it is, and the innocent people suffer while the real criminals are not punished. The comedy in his novels often comes from the contrast between what a character will accept and what the reader knows to be right; unlike Fielding and Jane Austen, he does not use a comic situation to make right something that was wrong or unfair.

Scoop[18] (1937), the story of a British reporter at a war in East Africa, has confusion after confusion: the wrong man is sent as the reporter, and after he has returned to England at the end of the war, a second (wrong) man is rewarded for something that the first (wrong) man did not do. By the time he wrote *Brideshead Revisited* (1945), however, a new note had entered Waugh's work. The first part of the novel, a picture of rich young men at university, is from the same world as his earlier books, but the later parts are much more serious and a religious theme has entered – that if a character does not play the part in life which has been arranged for him or her, he or she is failing God. His later group of three novels (*Men at Arms*, 1952; *Officers and Gentlemen*, 1955; and *Unconditional Surrender*[19], 1961) is also more serious, although there are comic moments. The main character, Guy Crouchback, is always trying to do his best for God and man, but always ends by doing something foolish. *The Loved One* (1948) is a very sharp satire on American attitudes to the treatment of the dead which is very much in the spirit of his earlier books, and contrasts European beliefs and behaviour with American ones, to great comic effect.

---

[18] *scoop*, an exciting news report made by one newspaper before any other papers publish it.
[19] *surrender*, to yield completely.

The detective novel is a form that became very popular towards the end of the nineteenth century, particularly through the 'Sherlock Holmes' stories of SIR ARTHUR CONAN DOYLE. In these books, each story is a puzzle, but the readers are given enough information to discover for themselves the answer to the mystery, or (more often) who the murderer is. In the twentieth century the most famous writer of detective stories is AGATHA CHRISTIE, whose long line of books began with *The Mysterious Affair at Styles* in 1920. Her early books have a Belgian detective, Hercule Poirot, as the hero, while the main character of the later books is Miss Marple, a quiet old English lady.

The spy novel (used by Conrad, Graham Greene and Anthony Burgess, among many others) has been taken in a new direction by JOHN LE CARRÉ. In Le Carré's work the personality (often a very complicated one) of the spy becomes much more interesting and important, and the situation in which he is spying reflects the political and international events of the real world. *The Spy Who Came In From The Cold* (1963) made him very famous, and his later novels of the British secret service, based around the character of George Smiley, are also very different from the traditional spy novel in that they are not merely concerned to tell a good story but also deal with themes (such as the claims of personal responsibility against those of national loyalty) explored by 'serious' novels.

GEORGE ORWELL wrote several novels in the 1930s, but his fame rests mainly on his later books and his political and critical writing. The heroes of his early novels (including *Burmese Days*, 1934; *Coming Up For Air*, 1939) share with Orwell himself the desire and ability to cut through lies and pretence to find out the truth about a situation or a person. Orwell was very conscious of the ways in which language could be used to hide the truth, and he shows how governments can use language to deceive the people in *Nineteen Eighty-Four* (1949). This book describes a future world where every word and action is seen and controlled by the state, which has developed a kind of television that can watch people in their own homes, and is changing the language so that the only words left are those for objects and ideas that the government wants the people to know about. For Orwell, the quality of a language suggests the quality of the society that uses it, so that a government controls a language in order to control completely the people who use it. This picture of the future, influenced by the hardships and dangers of the Second World War and the political events that followed it, is a dark despairing one. Orwell recognizes the important part that the state must play in a fair society, but he also feels that all human beings need to be able to be private sometimes so that they can be themselves.

Much of Orwell's best writing is political and he is certainly the most important political writer of the post-war years. He fought in the Spanish Civil War (1935–37) and wrote about his experiences in *Homage to Catalonia*, and for many years he wrote essays and articles for newspapers and magazines which were often on political subjects. One of the subjects that most interested him, and on which he wrote most often, was the relationship between literature and politics:

> To dislike a writer's politics is one thing. To dislike him because he forces you to think is another, not necessarily compatible with the first. But as soon as you start talking about 'good' and 'bad' writers you are tacitly appealing to literary tradition and then dragging in a totally different set of values. For what is a 'good' writer? Was Shakespeare 'good'? Most people would agree that he was. Yet Shakespeare is, and perhaps was even by the standards of his own time, a reactionary in tendency; and he is also a difficult writer, only doubtfully accessible to the common man.

Perhaps his most famous work is a political allegory, *Animal Farm* (1945), which tells the story of a political revolution that went wrong. The animals on a farm, led by the pigs, drive out their master Jones and take control of the farm, but the purity of their political ideas is soon destroyed, and they end by being just as greedy and dishonest as the farmer whom they drove out:

> Meanwhile life was hard. Once again all rations[A] were reduced, except those of the pigs and the dogs. A too rigid[B] equality in rations, Squealer explained, would have been contrary[C] to the principles[D] of Animalism. In any case he had no difficulty in proving to the other animals that they were *not* in reality short

of food, whatever the appearances might be. For the time being, certainly, it had been found necessary to make a readjustment[E] of rations (Squealer always spoke of it as a 'readjustment', never as a 'reduction') ... The animals believed every word of it. Truth to tell, Jones and all he stood for had almost faded out of their memories. They knew that life nowadays was harsh[F] and bare, that they were often hungry and often cold, and that they were usually working when they were not asleep. But doubtless it had been worse in the old days. They were glad to believe so.

[A] allowance of food　[B] strict　[C] against　[D] beliefs　[E] change　[F] hard

As we have seen, the intention driving many writers this century has been the wish to describe things as they really are without being influenced by tradition or convention. One of the early works of biography to attempt this was LYTTON STRACHEY's *Eminent Victorians*[20] (1918), which gave a very different picture of the people he described (including Queen Victoria) from the admiring portraits drawn in the last century. Strachey wanted to correct the public picture of famous people, who were always described as noble, honest, clever and brave, and to show that they were no more perfect than anyone else. His approach made him famous at the time and has been copied by many other writers of biography since.

The twentieth century has seen many books of travel and adventure, and one of the most famous in English is *The Seven Pillars*[21] *of Wisdom* by T. E. LAWRENCE, published in 1926, which is an account of his adventures in Arabian deserts during the First World War. It is more, however, than the story of one man's experiences; it is written in a very poetic style which includes reflections on man's nature as well as descriptions of battles and of the beauty of the desert across which Lawrence travelled:

> At sunset we reached the northern limit of that land and rode up a new level, higher than the old, of blue-black rock ... The rain had washed away the lighter dust below and between till

[20] *eminent Victorians*, famous people who lived in the time of Queen Victoria.
[21] *pillar*, a tall, thin, upright support (for a roof, etc.).

the stones, set closely side by side and as level as a carpet, covered all the face of the plain.

It was now very dark: a pure night enough, but the black stone underfoot swallowed the light of the stars . . . The flames of our fire went shining across the dark flat. It was two hours before the last group arrived, the men singing their loudest, partly to encourage themselves and their hungry animals over the ghostly plain, partly so that we might know them as friends. We wished their slowness slower, because of our warm fire.

One of the most interesting developments in the writing of the twentieth century is the greater number of women writers. Some of these deal with essentially the same subjects as men do, although they often are particularly interested in the feelings and consciousness of their characters (for example, in their different ways, Virginia Woolf and Iris Murdoch). The novels of IVY COMPTON-BURNETT (including *Brothers and Sisters*, 1929; *Parents and Children*, 1941; *A Heritage*[22] *and its History*, 1959) deal with the family, but in a very original way. The stories are told almost completely through conversation, and the picture of family life is one where the cruel and deceitful win, while the weak and honest lose. No force from inside or outside can change her characters; the bad are never punished and the good are never rewarded. In these novels, the traditions of the Victorian family have been drawn aside to show that the reality of their life is basically cruel and destructive.

During the century, many women novelists have wanted to write about the lives, problems and special concerns of women in the modern world, so that a group of novels have appeared which have women characters at their centre and are written very much from women's point of view.

DORIS LESSING's first novel, *The Grass is Singing* (1959), which is set in southern Africa, explores the mind of the wife of a poor white farmer there, and follows the events that lead to her destruction, while the main character in her group of novels called *Children of Violence* (which began in 1952) follows the main character, Martha Quest, as she tries to move away from the old ideas of the society in which she was

---

[22] *heritage*, something which one receives by right from an older person or people.

brought up, about politics and religion and the part to be played by women, and to live her life according to her own beliefs. *The Golden Notebook* (1962) is a powerful attempt to write honestly about women's lives and beliefs and the pressures that political and social events in twentieth-century life and society put on them. The outside world and the people in it are often seen as unfriendly and wishing to hurt the female characters – the men in the novel often hurt and damage the women because they themselves are weak. The reasons for this are often political – Doris Lessing is one of the most politically conscious of twentieth-century writers – but often also come from the characters' inability to tell the difference between the way things appear to be and the way they really are:

> He went off, taking me with him. I could feel part of myself leaving the house with him. I knew how he went. He stumbled[A] down the stairs, stood a moment before facing the street . . . He had left the devils behind him in my flat, and for a moment he was free. But I could feel the cold of loneliness coming from him. The cold of loneliness was all around me.
>
> [A] almost fell

MARGARET DRABBLE's main characters are also women, and they are often women whose intelligence is directed to study (at university, etc.) and not to their feelings or their knowledge of themselves or others. In *The Millstone*[23] (1965) a girl who has avoided any deep feelings or close relationships with other people finds that she is brought into the world of human feelings by her love for her child, while in *The Waterfall* (1969) the main character, a poet, who is unable at the beginning of the book to connect body and mind, is saved from the coldness of her life by sexual love, and is at last able to understand herself and her personality as a woman. *The Ice Age* (1977) presents a wider picture of an unhappy world in which the coldness of the spirit and the feelings that comes when people only live in one part of their personalities is shown as a danger to the whole of society.

From the 1960s onwards there has been an increasing interest in books written by and about women, and several publishing firms have been set up to meet this interest; an example is Virago Press, which as

[23] *millstone*, the heavy stone in a mill with which corn is crushed into flour.

Margaret Drabble

well as publishing new books (novels and others) about women and their experience of the world has also republished older books of special interest to women. Several important women writers from the first half of the century – among them REBECCA WEST, STORM JAMESON, ELIZABETH BOWEN and ROSAMOND LEHMANN – have found a new audience in this way. The works of younger women novelists such as EDNA O'BRIEN and MURIEL SPARK remain popular.

*2001: A Space Odyssey was made into a
well-known film*

Science fiction is generally described as stories based on developments
in science or technology – either existing developments, or fictional
developments of the future. Early science fiction falls into three main
areas:

1) the danger to man and the possibility of destruction if present
   scientific or technological developments are carried further;
2) what may happen after man has defeated the problems of war,
   disease and poverty – that man may be able to go beyond the limits
   of the human body and gain some of the qualities of machines;
3) although man may have lost something of natural life on earth (as
   in the second area above), he can explore the world of space.

Many writers who have been mentioned in connection with their
other work have also written science fiction; as has been already said,
many of the novels of H. G. Wells fall into this group. Wells was very
interested in the scientific advances of his age and looked ahead to
imagine what the results might be in the future. On the whole, he was
interested in the possibilities for good rather than in the disadvantages,
although he was conscious of the possible dangers, and many of his

novels present a struggle between two ways of life, the human and the non-human. E. M. Forster's short story *The Machine Stops* (1909) describes a world where the machines are in control; and ALDOUS HUXLEY, who also wrote several lighter novels of social satire, gave a picture in *Brave New World* (1932) of a society so heavily organized and controlled that the only way for people to be themselves lies in escape. George Orwell, in *Nineteen Eighty-Four*, and Anthony Burgess, in *A Clockwork Orange*, also give pictures of a future world, but their interest is less in the scientific advances that have been made than the purposes these are used for. Orwell is interested in the effect on the human personality and Burgess in the moral problems that change can bring. Kingsley Amis, as well as writing science fiction himself, has also written a book about the type of literature, called *New Maps of Hell* (1961), and in *The Four-Gated City* (1969) Doris Lessing also moves into the area of science fiction when she describes the world after it has been almost destroyed, and several of her later novels have also been in the area of science fiction.

As well as these writers, there are many others whose work has been mainly science fiction, for example JOHN WYNDHAM, who in *The Day of the Triffids* (1951) and *The Krakan Wakes* (1953) shows the world after society as we know it today has been completely destroyed (Triffids and Kraken are the names of creatures which he invented for the books). BRIAN ALDISS has written many books in this area, among them *Greybeard* (1964), which uses the same theme as John Wyndham, of a small group of people trying to stay alive when most of the world has been destroyed. Aldiss has also written *Barefoot in the Head* (1969), in which he uses language that is clearly influenced by James Joyce in *Finnegan's Wake* to express what is happening in a world that has gone through a war fought with drugs.

ARTHUR C. CLARKE has also written much science fiction, including *The City and the Stars* (1957), in which a whole society is created by one machine that organizes everything until a mistake leads to the creation of a man who fights the rest of the society. He also wrote *2001: A Space Odyssey*[24] (1968), which takes up the subject of exploration in space. The details of science fiction stories change and develop as scientific advances are made, but many of the themes remain the same.

[24] *odyssey*, a long adventurous journey.

A caricature of George Bernard Shaw

Chapter Fourteen

Twentieth-century drama

In the work of many twentieth-century English dramatists it is possible to see not only the products of the individual writer's ideas and experience, but also several general tendencies. This does not mean that the writers are members of a group, but that they share enough beliefs and concerns for their work to have several important things in common.

One of these loose groupings relates to the attempt to show on stage some parts of the daily lives of ordinary people in a realistic way that often contains social and political criticism. This type of play has a history at least as old as the century: the plays of JOHN GALSWORTHY, for example, which share the forms of the traditional well-made play, combine a description of social and political evils with great sympathy for the people who hopelessly and helplessly suffer them. In *Strife*[1] (1909) he shows the progress of a strike caused by both sides' refusal to change their demands, which is settled on exactly the same terms as were suggested at the beginning but which has caused huge suffering and hardship to the strikers' families. In *Justice* (1910) he shows the fate of a man who in a despairing attempt to escape from the miseries of his life writes a false signature on a cheque and has the rest of his life ruined by the 'justice' of those in power; at last, in despair, he kills himself.

GEORGE BERNARD SHAW was born in Ireland but spent most of his long adult life in England. An important aim of his many plays was to face his audiences with completely new points of view and ways of

[1] *strife*, trouble between people.

looking at themselves and the society they lived in. He enjoyed the shock and offence this often produced, particularly when his ideas were expressed with much wit. He delighted in saying and showing the opposite of what his audiences expected: *Arms and the Man* (1898), for example, presents as a sympathetic figure a soldier who doesn't want to fight, and in *The Devil's Disciple*[2] (1901) the man whom conventional society has thought of as evil and selfish is willing to sacrifice himself for others, while the minister of religion discovers that he should have been a soldier.

Several of Shaw's plays show in various ways the workings of his theory[3] of the 'Life Force', the power that drives people to value life as a great gift and fight for a better world, and that leads women, in particular, to want to have children so that life can be continued in them. The main character in *Man and Superman* (1903), which shows the working of this theory most clearly, says that a woman's real aim in life is to find the man that nature tells her is the right father for her children. The same theory influenced *Caesar and Cleopatra* (1901), in which Julius Caesar represents man at a high point of his intellectual development, and Cleopatra represents untamed natural passion. It can also be seen in *Major Barbara* (1905), when the heroine, a woman of strong personality and ideals, exchanges her belief in Christianity for that in the Life Force.

Shaw did not believe in Christianity or any other organized religion himself, and *Saint Joan* (1924), one of his best-known plays, presents the saint as a strong-minded woman of great energy and courage who possesses much of the Life Force within her and who is opposed and at last killed by the traditional powers of Church and State, to whom she had become a threat.

Pygmalion (1912) is particularly well known because it was the basis for the musical play and film *My Fair Lady*. In this story of the professor[4] who takes a flower-seller from the London streets and makes her into a grand lady, it is behaviour and not ways of talking that really shows the differences between the characters. For Eliza, the flower-seller, the most important thing in human relationships is that people

---

[2] *disciple*, someone who follows a leader closely.
[3] *theory*, a set of ideas based on reasoned argument which is intended to explain known facts or events.
[4] *professor*, the teacher at the head of a university department.

care about each other; for Professor Higgins, the most important thing is that they help each other to improve themselves. As in his many other plays, Shaw delights in showing opposing attitudes in sharp and witty language that often turn upside down the accepted opinion of his time. The prefaces[5] to his plays, which discuss their subjects and themes at greater length, as well as many other books, show the wide extent of his interest and concern on political, social and religious subjects as well as the language in which they are expressed.

The work of SEAN O'CASEY, like Galsworthy's, shows concern for innocent victims although the events that shape the lives of O'Casey's characters are more clearly political. O'Casey was an Irishman, and his best-known plays are set in the time of great events in Ireland earlier this century, but the events are always seen from the point of view of the ordinary people. *The Shadow of a Gunman* (1923) is set at the time of the Irish War of Independence, but events are shown as they affect the lives of the ordinary people, who suffer most from it. The play is written with humour as well as great sympathy for their sufferings.

Juno and the Paycock (1924) is set in the Irish Civil War, but the chief interest is in the main characters: Juno, a Dublin housewife, is trying to hold her family together against the forces that are trying to destroy it (lack of money, a weak drunken husband, a daughter who is deserted by the father of her child, and a son already wounded who is taken away at the end of the play to be shot as a spy). *The Plough and the Stars* (1926) deals with the Irish rising against the British in 1916. For O'Casey, it is always the women who suffer most from the realities of war while the men talk and dream and try to be heroes. The play gains much of its life and energy from the language of his characters, who are native to Dublin although their feelings are universal, as in Juno's lament for her dead son:

> What was the pain I suffered, Johnny, bringing you into the world to carry you to your cradle[A], to the pain I'll suffer carrying you out of the world to bring you to your grave! Mother of God, have pity on us all, and take away our hearts of stone and give us hearts of flesh! Take away this murdering hate and give us your own eternal[B] love!

[A] baby's bed   [B] endless

[5] *preface*, an introduction to a book in which the author explains why he or she wrote it.

Another Irish writer, J. M. SYNGE, was also concerned with describing the lives of ordinary people as they really were, but the group of people he chose to write about was a special one – the people of the Aran Islands, off the west coast of Ireland, which Synge visited often. His best-known play, *The Playboy of the Western World* (1907) caused fighting in the theatre when it was first performed in Dublin. The people of a small village admire a young stranger when he tells how he killed his cruel father, but turn against him when his father comes in search of him (saying that his son's blow only made him faint). It shows the moment when a son will no longer accept his father's power over him, and does so with a great delight in language and humour that gives a lively picture of the life of the people it describes.

ARNOLD WESKER is also concerned to show the realities of everyday life for ordinary people, but with a clearer note of social criticism. *The Kitchen* (1960) shows the kitchen of a large restaurant and the people who work in it. The play's real concern is not to show what they do in the kitchen so much as what the kitchen does to them: like all places of mass production, in Wesker's eyes, it makes them less than human.

His three plays *Chicken Soup with Barley* (1959), *Roots* (1959), and *I'm Talking about Jerusalem* (1960) show the lives of members of the same

A scene from Arnold Wesker's Roots, 1959

family from the 1930s to the 1950s. The first play shows a working-class Jewish family, the Kahns of London, and the way political and social events affect their idealism: by the end, all but the mother have been made bitter and selfish by the world in which they live. *Roots* shows the effect of the son of the Kahn family on the woman he plans to marry, who comes from the country. She has rejected her family's narrow way of looking at life but is not able to find a way for herself until the end of the play, when the shock of receiving his letter telling her that he will not marry her after all suddenly helps her to gain a real understanding of herself and confidence that she can express her own ideas. The last play of the three shows two members of the Kahn family who leave London for the country to live a simple life following traditional ways; in the end their attempt fails, but they are determined to go on trying to make for themselves the sort of life they want to lead.

Chips with Everything (1962) shows the British class system at work in the Air Force. A rich man's son wishes to be only an ordinary airman instead of an officer as part of his personal fight against his father rather than a fight against the class system. He, like his father, really wants power, and at the end of the play, after encouraging the other airmen to start a revolution against the class system (which achieves nothing), he returns to his own class and agrees to become an officer.

Wesker's later plays (including *Their Very Own and Golden City*, 1966, and *The Friends*, 1970) moved further away from a realistic representation of real life. Their common theme is the importance for individuals of avoiding the pressures created by the society in which they live and of finding their own standards of right and wrong.

TREVOR GRIFFITHS is also deeply interested in social themes, but his plays make clearer political statements than do Wesker's. *The Party* (1973) makes a play on words with its title; it is set at a party for members of Socialist[6] and Communist[7] political parties. It makes a bitter comparison between the comfortable life of the middle-class intellectual socialist who talks about the revolution but will do nothing for it, and an older man who has tried to live his life according to his political beliefs and has sacrificed everything for them.

---

[6] *Socialist*, someone who believes in state ownership of the means of production, etc.
[7] *Communist*, someone who believes in a classless society in which the state owns the means of production and shares the goods produced according to each person's need.

Comedians[8] (1975) shows six students at a night-class for comedians, and explores the connection between comedy and morality. It also explores the purpose of comedy, to free people from fear by making them laugh at the thing they are afraid of, and to encourage them to go out and do something to change the situation that produced the fear.

EDWARD BOND is less concerned with the daily details of people's lives and more with the rules of right and wrong that they have made for themselves. His plays are on a heroic scale, with the theme that the world (and therefore society) is badly organized and must be changed. In his plays man's self-destructiveness is often made clear in his violent actions.

Narrow Road to the Deep North (1968), set in ancient Japan, shows how a baby left to die becomes a cruel ruler, and asks whether the poet who saw the child and did nothing is responsible for all the pain and suffering that the ruler caused. The play also considers the effect of colonialism[9], both on those who rule and those who are ruled.

Lear (1971) is Bond's account of Shakespeare's tragedy *King Lear*, in which Lear's good daughter, Cordelia, is made evil and dishonest by achieving the power she set out to destroy. *Bingo* (1974) shows Shakespeare himself as an ill and dying man, returned to his home in the country after his success in London. There is a powerful comparison between Shakespeare the great artist and Shakespeare the man, who is a failure as a husband and a father and agrees to actions by the authorities that will harm the ordinary people.

The Fool (1975) is also about the life of an English poet; it is based on the story of John Clare, a poet in the eighteenth century who was kept in prison as a madman for many years. The play explores the mysterious relationship between pain of the mind and heart, and true poetic vision. This is a theme also explored in *The Woman* (1978), in which the main character gains new knowledge and understanding through great pain and suffering. Bond's world is often a cruel and bitter one, although there are touches of humour; but many things that have happened in the twentieth century are cruel and bitter, and Bond's work, like that of the other dramatists, can be said to reflect the world in which we all live.

[8] *comedian*, a person whose job (in a theatre, club etc.) is to make others laugh.

[9] *colonialism*, the situation when a group of people from one country live in and control part or all of another country.

Vladimir and Estragon in
Waiting for Godot

Samuel Beckett

A second area of concern in twentieth-century English drama is that of the individual's search for identity[10] in an unfriendly outside world, and the difficulty and fear of communicating with other individuals.

A famous example of this is the work of SAMUEL BECKETT, who was born in Ireland but has spent most of his adult life in France and has written many of his works in French before translating them into English. As a young man he was a friend of James Joyce (see p. 148) and like him is fascinated by words; but unlike Joyce he sees language as building a wall between human beings which stops them communicating. His play *Waiting for Godot* (1954) is one of the most influential works in English written this century. It takes away the surface detail from the situations it presents and shows their real nature; in the words of one critic, 'it describes the essence of the human condition'. The play shows two tramps,[11] Vladimir and Estragon, who are waiting for the arrival of the mysterious Godot to give their lives some purpose and direction. But Godot does not come, and may not even exist. The play shows the pain and fear as well as the humour of the two men as they despairingly try to use reason and argument to help them in a situation where reason is not enough. Of the two,

[10] *identity*, the real nature of a person.
[11] *tramp*, a person with no home or job, who goes from one place to another asking for food and money.

Estragon is more determined that they should wait for Godot as they have been told to do:

VLADIMIR: What are you suggesting? That we've come to the wrong place?
ESTRAGON: He should be here.
VLADIMIR: He didn't say for sure he'd come.
ESTRAGON: And if he doesn't come?
VLADIMIR: We'll come back tomorrow.
ESTRAGON: And then the day after tomorrow.
VLADIMIR: Possibly.
ESTRAGON: And so on.
VLADIMIR: The point is –
ESTRAGON: Until he comes.
VLADIMIR: You're merciless.

Endgame (1957) also shows characters in a closed situation which they continually fight against. As in *Waiting for Godot*, the surface details are cut to the bare essentials; it is set in no particular place, at no particular time, and the characters play games with words which they intend only to pass the time but which take on a meaning they had not thought of. *Krapp's Last Tape* (1959) has only one character, an old man sitting in a closed room with a tape recorder, playing the tapes he made at earlier points in his life and reflecting on the thoughts and impressions he had had as a younger man and the difference in his thoughts and feelings now. In *Happy Days* (1961) the main character is a woman, Winnie. The characters in Beckett's earlier plays were despairing and lost, fighting against the emptiness of their lives and their loss of hope: Winnie is resigned to her fate with a cheerfulness that is almost more frightening than their despair. The title of the play holds a bitter humour: she is determined to be happy because she will not face the terrible things that are happening to her. Her defence is that she will not allow herself to care; and for this reason, this has been described as Beckett's most despairing play.

Beckett is interested in those characters who refuse not only love but any real relationship with anyone else; they are lost and unhappy, and have only the pleasure of language left. Beckett's language is very carefully used, and there is much more humour in his plays than the

A production of Harold Pinter's The Caretaker *in 1980*

despair of their themes might suggest.

The plays of HAROLD PINTER also have as a central theme the impossibility of communication between characters in a closed situation, although in his early plays the closed situation is often a room whose comfort and safety is compared with the dangers of the world and the strangers outside.

The Birthday Party (1957) presents the closed, comfortable situation of a small lodging-house and the effect of the arrival of two mysterious strangers who have come to 'collect' one of the people living there. The feeling of danger is made stronger both by the suggestions of violence and the fact that the reason why the strangers have come to collect him is never fully explained. *The Caretaker* (1960) also presents a closed situation (two brothers in a house) and the arrival of a stranger (an old tramp), but in this case it is the stranger who is the victim. The suspicions increase as the uncertainty grows, the relationships between the characters change, but in spite of some touches of humour it is the sense of emptiness of the characters' lives that is probably the strongest impression left by the play.

In *The Homecoming* (1964) the danger comes from inside the home and the victim again comes from outside, although this time he is a member of the family: one of the sons returns from America with his wife and, after threats of violence, in the end loses his wife to the rest of his family. *No Man's Land* (1975) shows the meeting of two old men who had known each other when they were young; one is now rich and successful, while the other is in many ways a failure. In a sense they are enemies, although on the surface they meet as friends, and there is always a feeling of danger between them. ('No man's land' means an empty piece of land between two enemies or different countries.) In some ways it is the rich and successful man who is the real failure, because in his heart he is living in the 'no man's land' of no feelings and no hope.

In Pinter's work, as in Beckett's work, it is not only the words that are said that are important; the silences and the words which are not said are also important. Pinter has said that there are two sorts of silence – one where no word is spoken and the other where a flood of language is being used – and his plays reflect the difficulty of communication between people that this statement suggests.

A third general grouping in modern English drama can be seen in those plays in which language is not only the means by which the characters' feelings and beliefs are expressed but an important part of the play in its own right, particularly when it is used for a witty or comic effect to contrast with the seriousness of the theme beneath.

OSCAR WILDE's plays were a leading example of this type of drama at the end of the nineteenth century, and his work has had great effect on several writers in the twentieth. Wilde's comedies, of which *The*

Oscar Wilde's The Importance of Being Earnest

Importance of Being Earnest (1895) is the most famous, are carried along by the witty language, which often gains its comic effect by reversing completely what is usual or expected. Cecily, for example, hopes that Algernon (who has just told her he loves her) has not been leading a double life and pretending to be wicked when he was really good all the time: she would be very disappointed if he were not wicked after all. Algernon himself can also reverse the conventional way of looking at things:

> JACK: That is the whole truth, pure and simple.
>
> ALGERNON: The truth is rarely pure and never simple. Modern life would be very tedious[A] if it were either, and modern literature a complete impossibility.
>
> [A] boring

It is a world in which the appearance of things and people, and their reality, are always in contrast with each other, and these surprising contrasts are expressed in language of great wit and balance. Very often in Wilde's work, the manner in which ideas are expressed seems more important than their matter.

The plays of JOE ORTON may seem in a different world from that of Wilde's; Orton's are set in the 1960s, his characters are from the lower middle class in contrast to Wilde's ladies and gentlemen, and there are violent events in Orton's plays (*Entertaining Mr Sloane*, 1964; *Loot*, 1967) that are unthinkable in Wilde's. However, the comic effect of his works also comes from the contrast – the wide gap – between appearance and reality. The shocking events of his plays and the violence and greed of his characters are described in polite, lady-like language. Wilde's characters, however, knew how clever and witty they were; Orton's do not understand how laughable they are. In *Loot*, the detective Truscott is full of the importance which the authority of his job gives him, and demands that everything be done according to the rules; when one of the other characters asks for permission to get a photograph that may give useful information, Truscott makes a condition:

> FAY: Can't he fetch the photo?
>
> TRUSCOTT: Only if some responsible person accompanies[A] him.

HAL: You're a responsible person. You could accompany him.

TRUSCOTT: What proof have I got that I'm a responsible person?

DENNIS: If you weren't responsible you wouldn't be given the power to behave as you do.

^{A} goes with

Another writer for whom the use of language is of enormous importance in the the relationship between appearance and reality is TOM STOPPARD, who uses play on words to explore as well as express ideas about life and death, right and wrong, and the nature of man and the world. *Rosencrantz and Guildenstern are Dead* (1966) puts in the centre of the play two unimportant characters from *Hamlet*. We see the characters in Stoppard's play at the moment that they have left the stage in *Hamlet*, and they leave Stoppard's stage to return to Shakespeare's play. The two men play games to pass the time and wonder what will happen next and what their fate will be (which we in the audience know already from *Hamlet*). Stoppard plays with the meaning and sound of words, and so explores the gap between words and their meanings to different people, between what is said and what is intended.

Jumpers (1972) weaves together the story of a philosopher[12] who is married to an actress with the hunt for a murderer. Stoppard cleverly uses the ability of the theatre to present contrasting ideas, not only through different characters but in the gap between their description of a situation and what we know of the situation by other means.

Travesties (1974) uses *The Importance of Being Earnest* as its starting-point; some of the characters are the same and so are many of their remarks and the events which happen. It is set in Zurich in 1917, and shows three different types of revolutionary[13] – Lenin (in politics); James Joyce (in literature); and Tristan Tzara (in art) – all seen through the eyes of an unimportant official at the British Consulate[14].

[12] *philosopher*, someone who studies the nature of existence, reality, knowledge, etc.
[13] *revolutionary*, a person who tries to bring about great social change, or new ways of thinking or acting.
[14] *Consulate*, the official building or offices of one country's government in a foreign city.

Stoppard presents each of the three revolutionaries in turn, and shows us events from the three different points of view. Then he reminds us that everything is being seen through the memory of an old man who may not remember correctly, so that the contrast between the events that are shown on stage and what really happened – between appearance and reality – is made clear. The play also considers the nature of art and the part to be played by an artist in society, especially in changing society. At the end of the play, the official, who is now over eighty years old, reflects on what he has learned:

> I learned three things in Zurich during the war. I wrote them down. Firstly, you're either a revolutionary or you're not, and if you're not you might as well be an artist as anything else. Secondly, if you can't be an artist, you might as well be a revolutionary.... I forget the third thing.

Some critics have suggested that Stoppard enjoys the comic surface of his plays so much that he does not give enough attention to the human feelings and concerns beneath. This is not true even in his earlier plays – the basis of *Rosencrantz and Guildenstern are Dead* , for example, is the understanding that the fact that their deaths matter so little to Hamlet is something that should have mattered to Shakespeare. His later plays show an even clearer and stronger human concern. *Every Good Boy Deserves Favour* (1977), with an equally comic surface, has as its main character a Russian political prisoner whom the authorities are attempting to prove mad, so that Stoppard uses the contrasts between appearance and reality here both for comic effect and also with a serious purpose.

English drama in the twentieth century has seen other attempts at new forms. One of the most interesting was that of T. S. ELIOT, who was better known as a poet (see p. 187), and whose three plays in verse, (*Murder in the Cathedral*, 1935; *The Family Reunion*, 1939; *The Cocktail Party*, 1950) show an attempt to copy in English the form of the plays of ancient Greece and Rome. The first of these, which describes the events leading to the murder of the English saint Thomas à Becket, is probably the most successful; the other two plays, which both use stories taken from ancient Greek tragedy in modern form, explore the feelings of bitterness and failure which Eliot sees as part of human relationships today.

Throughout the century there have been well-written plays in the traditional style which, although they may have a serious purpose, are written to entertain rather than to explore deep subjects.

The plays of J. B. PRIESTLEY were very popular when they were first performed and are still produced today; his best-known plays share an interest in the way we understand time. *Time and the Conways* (1937) moves the time of the events of the play from the past to the present and back to the past again, so that the audience can see the characters in their present situation and its contrast with their earlier hopes and intentions. *An Inspector*[15] *Calls* (1946) shows how each member of a family slowly understands that he or she is responsible because a girl who knew them all in different ways has killed herself.

TERENCE RATTIGAN is another well-known writer of traditional and successful plays. His work extends from light comedy, as in *French Without Tears* (1936) to more serious plays such as *The Winslow Boy* (1946) about the effect on his family of a schoolboy who is accused of stealing, at the beginning of the century, and *The Deep Blue Sea* (1952) about a married woman whose lover has left her and who attempts to kill herself.

JOHN OSBORNE became famous in 1956 when his play *Look Back in Anger* presented a new type of hero who became known as 'the angry young man' and had a great influence on drama written in the next few years. The hero was new in his fight against the society he lived in and the anger which its pressures made him feel, but the play was more traditional in form and approach than references to 'the new drama' at the time might suggest. Osborne's later plays, including *Luther* (1961) and *A Patriot For Me* (1965), are set in very different times and places – the first is in Germany is the sixteenth century, while the second is in Austria at the beginning of this century – but still have as their main character a man who cannot fit into the society of his time and who fights against it. Much of his work suggests that the world was better in the past than it is now, and *Watch It Come Down* (1975), with its theme of the values of a dying world under attack from the new one, makes this particularly clear.

[15] *inspector*, a police officer of middle rank.

PETER SHAFFER's plays also often have at their centre men whose beliefs and behaviour make them different from the people around them. *The Royal Hunt of the Sun* (1964) shows the battle of civilisations between the native society of South America and the Spanish who conquered it through the characters of the Inca king (who is also a god to his people) and the Spanish general; they are from two different worlds of experience, and the world of the Inca king has been conquered and will be destroyed by a different civilisation. *Equus* (1973) studies the battle between a boy who has blinded some horses on the farm where he worked and the psychiatrist[16] who is trying to find out why he did it. The psychiatrist comes to understand that his own life is poor in comparison with the boy's, who still has the ability to feel passion and wonder, and he comes to think that if he 'cures' the boy of the feelings that led him to act so cruelly he will have taken away from him the quality that made his life worth living.

ALAN AYCKBOURN is one of the most successful writers of comic plays; he takes the traditional form of the middle-class comedy to consider what makes his characters behave as they do. *Absurd Person Singular* (1973), through social comedy, shows the horror of human beings who are completely tied up in themselves and their social habits, while *Absent Friends* (1975) shows the thoughtless cruelty of members of a family to each other. A further consideration of family relationships is given in his most ambitious work, *The Norman Conquests* (1974), which is formed by three plays set in different parts of the same house with the same characters at the same time. His plays have moved from lighter comedies (though often with sharp social satire) to a deeper, more despairing study of the cruelty of people who are too concerned with themselves and the polite rituals of their lives to notice the personalities, needs and hopes of the people around them.

Television has played an important part in bringing drama to a much wider audience – many of the writers mentioned here, including Griffiths, Pinter and Stoppard, have written original work for television, and the stage plays of many others have been shown on television as well. This has had the effect of attracting the interest of people who might earlier have seldom gone to the theatre, and, because television can be a more realistic form than the stage, has often affected the approach of the dramatist to his material.

[16] *psychiatrist*, a doctor who works with diseases of the mind.

William Butler Yeats as a young man

Chapter Fifteen

Twentieth-century poetry

The history of English poetry in the twentieth century tends to support the frequent remark that poetry is essentially a private art form. Certainly, poets are often influenced by other poets, and those who live through the same social and political events may well share a common outlook on them, but in the end each poet works as a private and separate person who makes his or her own world from his or her own deep concerns. Necessarily, therefore, the story of English poetry in the twentieth century is very much a story of individual figures.

The great figure in the poetry of the early part of the century was W. B. YEATS, whose work covered fifty years: his first poems were published in 1889 and his last were written in 1939. He was Irish, and when he began writing an important concern of his poetry was to show and honour the nature and character of Ireland and the Irish people, by writing about the traditions and history of the Irish nation. In his later work his themes became more universal; his main subject was the way in which the world and the people in it are divided, and how they can be made whole. In his poem *An Irish Airman Foresees His Death*, the airman knows he will die in a war (the First World War) which does not affect his own country and will not make any difference to the lives of the people he cares about in his village in Ireland, so that he does not fight because the law or a sense of duty tell him he must, but rather because of the pleasure of the danger and excitement of fighting in the air:

> I balanced all, brought all to mind;
> The years to come seemed waste of breath,
> A waste of breath the years behind,
> In balance with this life, this death.

In one of Yeats's last poems he remembers the themes and stories of his early poems and plays in verse, and their grand heroic characters, and recognizes that he was attracted by their appearance and not by the reality that lay behind them:

> Players and painted stage took all my love,
> And not those things that they were emblems[A] of.
> [A] signs

Now, he says, he must return to the unheroic place where they all began, and not try to climb above them on a ladder of great themes and grand language:

> Now that my ladder's gone
> I must lie down where all the ladders start,
> In the foul[A] rag-and-bone[B] shop of the heart.
> [A] very dirty   [B] old clothes and rubbish

His later poetry uses plainer language, and is often more honest – and more painful in its description of human nature – than the poetry he wrote as a young man.

THOMAS HARDY is better known as a novelist (see p. 131), but he wrote poetry throughout his long life (he died in 1928 aged 88) and thought of it as more important than his novels. He wrote nearly a thousand shorter poems, and a long drama in verse, *The Dynasts*, which

Thomas Hardy

took thirty years to write, was published between 1904 and 1908. His
poetry does not suggest (as some of Yeats's later work does) that life is a
bitter tragedy; Hardy knows that life is hard, but also that man has the
strength to bear its hardness and go on living. His poetry shows great
joy in the natural beauty of the world, and also in the sudden touch of
humour in events – although the humour is sometimes bitter – that
helps man to go on living through hardship and suffering. In one poem
he describes how a young boy at a railway station feels sudden pity for
a man being taken to prison by a policeman, and shows his sympathy
for him in the only way he can, by playing him a tune to amuse him:

> And the man in the handcuffs[A] suddenly sang
>   With grimful[B] glee[C],
>   'This life so free
>   Is the thing for me!'
> And the constable[D] smiled and said no word,
> As if unconscious of what he heard,
> And so they went on till the train came in –
> The convict[E], and the boy with the violin.[F]

[A] metal rings to fasten the hands   [B] determined   [C] enjoyment   [D] policeman
[E] prisoner   [F] musical instrument

Here there is great irony in the words of the song that the boy has
chosen to play for a man who is clearly not free, but there is also human
warmth and sympathy between the boy and the convict as they play
and sing together.

Hardy's descriptions of human hardship and suffering are often
those of a man who can look at misery from a distance: the poets of the
First World War (1914–18) have an altogether sharper and more
painful view of the suffering caused by one man to another.

The romantic and patriotic view of many soldiers at the beginning
of the war is reflected in one of the most famous poems of RUPERT
BROOKE, who saw death for a soldier as a sacrifice that should be given
gladly for his country:

> If I should die, think only this of me,
> That there's some corner of a foreign field
> That is for ever England.

A patriotic poster of the First World War

As the fighting continued, however, and men came to know more of the realities of war, their understanding and feelings towards it changed.

SIEGFRIED SASSOON fought in France, and much of his anger is directed against the pointlessness of war, and against the senior officers who do not seem to realize the death and destruction – which could often have been avoided – that their orders will cause to the men they command. He also hated the patriotic satisfaction of the people at home who believed the heroic stories that the government told them about the war and did not want to know about the misery and suffering of the men who fought. In a poem to the women of England, he criticizes them because:

> You love us when we're heroes, home on leave[A],
> Or wounded in a mentionable place,
> [A] holiday

and says that they will not listen to accounts of what the war is really like, nor feel any human sympathy for those whose lives are broken and ruined by it:

> You can't believe that British troops 'retire'[A],
> When hell's last horror breaks them, and they run,
> Trampling[B] the terrible corpses[C] – blind with blood.
>   O German mother dreaming by the fire
>   While you are making socks to send your son
>   His face is trodden[D] deeper in the mud.

[A] run away   [B] stepping on   [C] dead bodies   [D] pressed down by feet

WILFRED OWEN is possibly the best-known English poet of the First World War. He shares with Sassoon the wish to describe what the war was really like to the people at home in order for them to understand its horror and the suffering of the soldiers. He refuses to accept the romantic patriotism of Rupert Brooke – the war, he points out, is fought by real men who bleed and die, not by heroes who are more than human – and he describes the idea that it is noble and right to die for one's country as 'the old lie'. His poems show very powerfully the discomfort, danger and pain of the soldiers, and the permanent damage which the war did to their minds and happiness. At the time when the official attitude of the British Army suggested that their enemies were hardly human beings, he wrote one of his most famous poems, *Strange Meeting*, in which he imagines a meeting in hell with an enemy soldier he has killed who reminds him of their common humanity:

> Whatever hope is yours
> Was my life also.

'Gassed' – a painting by J. S. Sargent

Owen also wrote of the men whose bodies would carry the marks of war for the rest of their lives, in his poem *Disabled*[1]:

> Now he will spend a few sick years in institutes[A],
> And do what things the rules consider wise,
> And take whatever pity they may dole[B].
> Tonight he noticed how the women's eyes
> Passed from him to the strong men that were whole.
> How cold and late it is! Why don't they come
> And put him into bed? Why don't they come?
>
> [A] hospitals   [B] give out

ISAAC ROSENBERG's experience of life both before and during the war was different from that of the other poets mentioned here; they were from the middle or upper classes (and were officers in the war) while he came from a working-class family and served as an ordinary soldier. For this reason he had much less of a formal education than they did, and this is reflected in the language of his poetry as well as the events it described. His language has great life and energy; it does not look back to the models and traditions that had been developed over the years, but gives the feeling that it had been forced into new forms to communicate a new experience. In one of his poems he describes how a soldier, at the moment of death, hears the sound made by the wheels of the cart in which Rosenberg is riding:

> His dark hearing caught our far wheels
> And the choked[A] soul stretched weak hands
> To reach the living word the far wheels said. . . .
> So we crashed round the bend,
> We heard his weak scream,
> We heard his very last sound,
> And our wheels grazed[B] his dead face.
>
> [A] fighting for breath   [B] touched

Brooke, Sassoon, Owen and Rosenberg all fought in the First World War and all were killed except Sassoon, who was badly wounded.

---

[1] *disabled*, someone whose body has been permanently hurt.

GERARD MANLEY HOPKINS wrote his poems between 1875 and 1889 (the year of his death), but they were not published until 1918. They became increasingly well known in the 1920s and 1930s and had great influence on many poets writing then. Hopkins was a priest, and the themes of his poetry concern the relationship of man to God and the problem of suffering in a world created by God, as well as delight in God's creation of the natural world. After his first poems he did not use traditional forms of rhyme and rhythm but developed his own, known as 'sprung rhythm', which depended on the counting of syllables[2] and the sound-patterns of the words, in a way which reflects the patterns of Old English poetry and of Milton's *Samson Agonistes*. One of his early, and simpler, poems presents a woman giving her reasons for becoming a nun[3] as her wish to find a safe place in a religious life, away from the noise and confusion of the rest of the world:

> I have desired to go
>   Where springs not fail,
> To fields where flies no sharp and sided hail[A],
>   And a few lilies blow.[B]
>
> And I have asked to be
>   Where no storms come,
> Where the green swell[C] is in the havens[D] dumb,
>   And out of the swing of the sea.

[A] frozen rain   [B] flower   [C] movement of water   [D] safe place

One of the best-known figures in the second quarter of this century was T. S. ELIOT, who was born in America but spent most of his adult life in England. He writes as a man living through the years after the First World War in which men's lives had been lost or damaged, their hopes destroyed and promises broken, and he sees poetry and ceremony as forces that can give meaning to the emptiness and confusion of the modern world. Some of the references to ceremony in his poetry come from the Christian church, but others are taken from much earlier beliefs in ceremonies that brought life and therefore hope back to a dry,

---

[2] *syllable*, part of a word said as one unit, *e.g.* the word *syllable* has three syllables.

[3] *nun*, a woman member of a group who lives apart from the world to follow a religious life.

dead, hopeless world. He gives great importance to the forces that make it possible for spiritual, as well as physical, life to continue.

The Waste Land (published in 1922) is a long, highly complex poem which brings together a group of characters as different in kind and time as a modern typist and a blind priest of ancient Greece who can see the future. It brings together the ancient beliefs in the circularity of the natural world's movement through life and death to new life, with the Christian belief in spiritual life after physical death. Much of the picture of human unhappiness in the poem comes from the fact that the characters cannot understand the meaning of their own experiences. Eliot sees the root of the modern world's unhappiness and confusion as the fact that people today cannot bring together the different areas of their experience – cultural, sexual and religious as well as the everyday physical world – to make a complete and healthy whole. Since Eliot's aim is to bring together a great variety of human voices and experiences, the different parts of his poem use many different styles – here, for example, is the everyday voice of one woman advising another to get herself a set of false teeth before her husband comes home from the war:

> Now Albert's coming back, make yourself a bit smart[A].
> He'll want to know what you done with that money he gave you
> To get yourself some teeth. He did, I was there:
> You have them all out, Lill, and get a nice set,
> He said, I swear I can't bear to look at you.
> [A] attractive

In contrast with this is the picture of the emptiness of spirit and feelings when Eliot considers the condition of man:

> What are the roots that clutch[A], what branches grow
> Out of this stony rubbish? Son of man,
> You cannot say or guess, for you know only
> A heap of broken images[B], where the sun beats
> And the dead tree gives no shelter, the cricket[C] no relief
> And the dry stone no sound of water.
> [A] hold tightly   [B] pictures or objects   [C] small insect

The aim of his other great work, *Four Quartets* (1944), is to show different ways of experiencing God and reality in different times, so that here the force that will give wholeness and purpose to man's life and mind is that of religion. By showing different kinds of time (through the lives of different people, through universal history and through sudden moments when truth about life and God is made clear) the poem is saying strongly that in the middle of the confusion and suffering of the modern world, timeless values still exist and can still be touched.

The years during which Eliot was writing saw many new writers making experiments with language in trying to communicate the reality of the new world. EDITH SITWELL, one of the most interesting of these writers, puts great importance on the patterns of sound in her poems. Her picture of life is one in which the forces of darkness and light are fighting for the world; true Christian feeling can bring light, but man more often chooses the darkness, as in her poem after the atomic bomb was dropped:

> The living blind and seeing Dead together lie
> As if in love ... There was no more hating then,
> And no more love: Gone is the heart of Man.

Of the group of English poets whose work became well known in the 1930s, W. H. AUDEN is the most famous and in many ways the most typical. His early work shows a concern for the important political and social events, and (in contrast with the distance that a poet like Eliot puts between himself and the age) a wish to become part of them. He saw changes in the forms and subjects of literature as a way of helping political and social change, and in some poems he writes directly about political events and their effect on private lives, as in poems on the Spanish Civil War (in the middle of the 1930s) and on the beginning of the Second World War in 1939:

> I sit in one of the dives[A]
> On Fifty-Second Street,
> Uncertain and afraid,
> As the clever hopes expire[B]
> Of a low dishonest decade[C];
> Waves of anger and fear

Circulate over the bright
And darkened lands of the earth,
Obsessing our private lives.
[A] bars   [B] die   [C] ten years

During the Second World War he went to live in America, and by the
end of the war he had lost much of his earlier hope that the world could
be changed and made better by decisive human action (political
action influenced by literature). After this time his poetry became in
many ways more personal and, increasingly, looking for spiritual
qualities in the life around him.

His poems often communicate a strong sense of the realities of
everyday life; he writes, for example, of how suffering and death can
happen for one man while someone else is eating or opening a window
or just walking dully along, and how a party that seems to the staff of
an Embassy to be boring and ordinary can mean war and death for the
countries whose fate depends on them:

And on the issue[A] of their charm depended
A land laid waste, with all its young men slain,[B]
The women weeping and its towns in terror.
[A] result   [B] killed

Auden also wrote many lyric poems, of which this early example is one
of the best known:

Lay your sleeping head, my love,
Human on my faithless arm;
Time and fevers burn away
Individual[A] beauty from
Thoughtless children, and the grave
Proves the child ephemeral[B]:
But in my arms till break of day
Let the living creature lie,
Mortal[C], guilty, but to me
The entirely beautiful.
[A] special   [B] living only for a short time   [C] certain to die

Two other poets who became known in the 1930s were LOUIS MACNEICE and CECIL DAY LEWIS. The poems of MacNeice deal with personal experiences as well as with political events and their results, while Day Lewis's best work is related to social themes, as in his song for the child of poor parents:

The stars in the bright sky
Look down and are dumb
At the heir[A] of the ages
Asleep in a slum.[B]

Thy[C] mother is crying,
Thy dad's on the dole[D],
Two shillings a week is
The price of a soul.

[A] person who will receive something   [B] poor, dirty house   [C] your
[D] money given by the State

The poets of the Second World War (1939–45) were very different from those of the First World War. In the years between the wars, the world had become a sadder and darker place for many people, and the poets of the Second World War did not go to fight with the same hopes as those of the First World War. Neither did they feel that their job was to warn and inform the people at home, since in this war people who were not fighting knew what the war was like and many of them suffered as much as the men and women who fought it: the time for heroic patriotism was over for ever. ROY FULLER, watching the old systems being destroyed in the war (he described it: 'The ridiculous empires break like biscuits') envied the poets of the past, whose choice of moral positions he felt to be greater than his:

I envy not only their talents[A]
And fertile[B] lack of balance,
But in the appearance of choice
In their sad and fatal voice.

[A] ability   [B] producing good things

Among the poets of this time there is often a sense of tiredness, of things being worn out, and of helplessness in the face of world events which they had no power to change or influence, so that the strongest poems are often those which describe personal experiences rather than world events. One of the best poems of KEITH DOUGLAS, for example, describes how he found the picture of a girl and a book with the message *Vergissmeinicht* (do not forget me) on the body of a dead German soldier:

> For here the lover and the killer are mingled[A]
> Who had one body and one heart,
> And death, who had the soldier singled[B],
> Has done the lover mortal hurt.
>
> [A] joined   [B] chosen

The language of most poets of the Second World War is often plain and simple, seeming almost dull in a way that reflects their dulled acceptance of world events they were powerless to change. The language of DYLAN THOMAS (whose first poems were published in 1934) is completely different: full of life, energy and feeling, with great strength and power. He was born and brought up in Wales, and Welsh traditions of the power of the spoken word, especially in matters of religion, are reflected strongly in his poetry. His work praises and delights in natural forces: the life of nature and the countryside, the forces of birth, sex and death, and the powerful feelings that they create. One of his most famous poems was written to his father as he lay dying; his father had been very powerful in the expression of his ideas and feelings, and it hurt Thomas to see that the old man could not use that power to fight his coming death:

> Do not go gentle into that good night:
> Old age should burn and rave[A] at close of day;
> Rage[B], rage against the dying of the light.
>
> And you, my father, there on that sad height,
> Curse, bless me now with your fierce tears, I pray;
> Do not go gentle into that good night,
> Rage, rage against the dying of the light.
>
> [A] talk wildly   [B] fight angrily

He wrote, he said, not for fame or money or influence, but to touch and show people their own human feelings. Yet he knew well that the forces of life are stronger than the forces of art, and many of those he wrote for might not listen. He wrote, he said,

> For the lovers, their arms
> Round the griefs of the ages,
> Who pay no praise or wages
> Nor heed[A] my craft[B] or art.

[A] pay attention to   [B] skill

Thomas also wrote a play, *Under Milk Wood* (finished in 1953 shortly before his death) which was first performed on radio but has since been also acted on stage. It shows a day in the life of a small Welsh village, with its secrets, ironies, goodness, wickedness, foolishness and humour. Its approach is best described in the words of the character who is weakest in respect of traditional morals but strongest in her love of life: 'Isn't life a terrible thing, thank God!'

TED HUGHES, whose work was first published in 1957, is also concerned with strong and sometimes violent forces of nature, but he writes with great powers of imagination as if from inside the birds and animals who are the subjects of many of his poems. He uses the qualities connected with them in traditional stories as well as observation of how they act in real life to build up a picture of the essential character of the bird or animal and the part it plays in the natural world. He has written several times about the hawk, a powerful bird which catches and eats birds and animals smaller than itself, and one of these poems in particular catches the strength and violence of the bird:

> I kill where I please because it is all mine.
> My manners are tearing off heads, the allotment[A] of death.
>
> The sun is behind me.
> Nothing has changed since I began;
> My eye has permitted no change.
> I am going to keep things like this.

[A] share

Throughout twentieth-century English poetry there has also been, in addition to the violence, bitterness and emptiness that are the themes of many writers, a line of poems expressing gentleness, peace and a love of quietness and things remaining as they are. ROBERT GRAVES has had a long poetic career – his first book of poetry was published in 1917 when he was twenty-two – and he is also well known as a prose writer, particularly on historical subjects. Many of his poems are love poems, and many more have as their central subject the relationship between men and women, and how the lost sense of innocence and wonder can be brought back to human relationships. These poems see physical love between men and women as representing the emotion that brings life to the world:

> She tells her love while half asleep
>> In the dark hours,
>>> With half words whispered low;
> As earth stirs in her winter sleep
>> And puts out grass and flowers,
>>> Despite[A] the snow
>>> Despite the falling snow.
>
> [A] in spite of

R. S. THOMAS, whose poems first attracted attention in the late 1950s and early 1960s, falls in some ways into the tradition of British poets who have written about the country, but his attention is often directed to the hardships of country life. He writes of the traditional country landscapes – the sheep on a hill, the cottages, the farmer in the fields – and points out that the scene is delightful only from a distance; when you get closer you realize that the sheep are diseased, the cottages are falling into ruins and the hardness and discomfort of his life has given the farmer an illness which will kill him. R. S. Thomas is a minister of religion and behind his poems is a sense that the hardness of life can only be made bearable by love of man and love of God, since qualities of mind alone are not enough. He writes of the

> Emptiness of the bare mind
> Without knowledge, and the frost[A] of
> Knowledge where there is no love.
> [A] frozen condition

PHILIP LARKIN is probably the best-known poet writing today in this tradition of quietness. He is strongly influenced by Hardy and, like him, looks back to the past with a sense of what has been lost. Larkin represents a group of poets who turned away, in the 1950s and 60s, from the influence of Dylan Thomas and the idea that the aim of poetry should be to express high emotion and the deepest feelings and forces of nature. Their subjects tend to be smaller and their language more clearly controlled; in much of this poetry there is a sense that reality is dull and unattractive but that living through a dream is equally impossible. Real happiness seems only to have happened in the past, as in Larkin's poem on hearing a bird of spring sing outside his window at the end of winter:

> It will be spring soon,
> It will be spring soon –
> And I, whose childhood
> Is a forgotten boredom
> Feel like a child
> Who comes on a scene
> Of adults reconciling[A]
> And can understand nothing
> But the unusual laughter
> And starts to be happy.
>
> [A] becoming friendly again after a quarrel

PETER PORTER is an Australian who went to England in the early 1950s and whose first poems were published in the 1960s. His work is often sharply satirical, full of realistic details of material objects and the appearance of things and people, but also has a deeper and more universal quality since he is always conscious of the presence of death, a force that man cannot fight against:

> and if we shout
> at the gods, they send us the god of death
> who is immortal[A] and who cannot read.
>
> [A] living for ever

STEVIE SMITH's voice as a poet is clear and unmistakeable; from her first work (published in 1937) to the last poems written just before her death in 1971 her style and subjects are completely her own. The poems seem simple, almost as if written by a child, on the surface; they argue with God, are rude about people she dislikes (especially those who act cruelly, either to other people or animals), and give sharp and critical descriptions of how people behave to each other. They are often very funny, but there is also sadness at the loneliness and unhappiness of some lives, as in her poem on the man drowning at sea who waved his arms to the people on land to show them that he needed help – but they thought he was only waving to say hello:

> Poor chap[A], he always loved larking[B]
> And now he's dead.
> It must have been too cold for him his heart gave way
> They said.
>
> Oh no no no, it was too cold always
> (Still the dead one lay moaning)
> I was much too far out all my life,
> And not waving but drowning.
> [A] man   [B] joking

Stevie Smith

Some of the most interesting poetry published since 1970 has been written by poets from Northern Ireland and some of the best poems have been written by SEAMUS HEANEY. In his early poems he writes of the countryside and of the natural world in a way that suggests he has been influenced by R. S. Thomas and Ted Hughes when he writes of his childhood in the country and its history. His later poems move from private history to the public events of the past and how they have influenced the present political and military situation in Northern Ireland. In one of his early poems he writes of his father and grandfather, and the skill they showed in using a spade when they were working in the fields; he is a writer and so his trade is different from theirs, but he would like to show as much skill with his pen as they did with their spades. Even here, however, there is a sense of threat: he describes his pen as fitting between his fingers and thumb as smoothly and tightly as a gun. In his later poems he describes a life where the use of guns, and the suffering they cause, is part of everyday reality, and where the humour of the remarks written on walls has a bitter edge:

> Is there a life before death? That's chalked up
> In Ballymurphy. Competence^A with pain,
> Coherent^B miseries, a bite and sup^C,
> We hug our little destiny^D again.
> ^{A} managing ^{B} understandable ^{C} drink ^{D} fate

Here the ironic change to the usual question 'Is there life after death?' gives a point to his description of a life where pain and misery have become part of the ordinary quality of life. Heaney is attempting to go beyond the daily events of the life around him, hard and painful as they often are, and to discover the forces below his country's history that can bring back life and hope.

Glossary of literary terms

allegory   a story which teaches a lesson because the people and places in it stand for other ideas. An example is John Bunyan's *Pilgrim's Progress* (see page 67).

alliteration   repeating a sound or a letter, especially at the beginning of words, in poetry: *e.g.* 'Five *m*iles *m*eandering with a *m*azy *m*otion ...' (see page 8).

assonance   repeating a vowel sound, often in the middle of words, in poetry: *e.g.* p*a*le/br*a*ve.

autobiography   the written account of a person's own life (see page 136).

ballad   originally a song for dancers, then in mediaeval times a simple poem with short stanzas telling a story. Some Romantic poets of the 19th century also wrote ballads (see page 91).

biography   the written account of someone else's life (see page 61).

blank verse   any verses, especially iambic pentameters (see *metre*), that do not rhyme. Used by Marlowe, Shakespeare, Milton and many other poets, this is the most characteristic English form (see page 23).

caricature   a way of drawing or writing which makes the special features of a person or group stronger, so that they are ridiculous.

chorus   in Greek drama the chorus watched the action of the play and told the story. The modern meaning can be simply a group of people other than the hero or heroine.

chronicle   a history of events year by year – *e.g.* the *Anglo-Saxon Chronicle* in Old English (see page 12).

classic   a) a work that is recognized as a great work: *e.g. Dickens' novels are some of the classics of English literature.*
b) ancient Greek or Latin literature: *e.g. We studied classics at university.*
c) writing influenced by ancient Greek and Latin literature: *e.g. Eighteenth century poets preferred classical forms.*
(*adjective:* **classical**)

comedy   something that is funny. A comedy usually means a play with a light happy story.
(*adjective:* **comic**)

couplet   two lines of verse that rhyme.

crisis   the most important part of a play, when the action takes an important turn and the feelings of the audience are strongest (see page 45).

dialogue   conversation between two or more people in a book, a play, etc.

diary   a written record of daily events. The most famous diary in English was written by Samuel Pepys (see page 69).

drama   a) any kind of work written to be performed on the stage, including comedies, tragedies, etc.
b) something exciting or important that happens. (*adjective:* **dramatic**)

edition   the printing of a book, often with changes made in second editions.

elision   leaving out a vowel or a syllable, or running two vowels together, to make the correct metre in a line of verse.

ellipsis   leaving out words which give the full sense: *e.g.* '*In wit* [he was] *a man:* [in] *simplicity* [he was] *a child.*' (Pope)

enjambement   running on the sense of one line of poetry to the next:
e.g. I have lived long enough. My way of
                            life
Is fall'n into the sear, the yellow leaf
(*Macbeth*)

epic   a long narrative poem in the grand style, often praising heroic adventures.

elegy   a poem of mourning for someone who is dead. Milton's 'Lycidas' was an elegy to his friend who drowned. Gray's 'Elegy in a Country Churchyard' is a sad poem about mankind's mortality (see page 75).

epigram   a short, funny, sharp poem or remark. Oscar Wilde was famous for his witty epigrams.

epilogue   an ending, or an extra part after the end of a book or play. Some of Shakespeare's plays have an epilogue addressed to the audience.

epitaph   something written on a tombstone, or a poem about someone after their death.

essay   a short prose work that is not fiction, often showing the writer's own ideas on a subject (see page 31).

fable   a legend; a story which tries to teach something.

fantasy   an imaginative work that might have no basis in the real world; something imagined* or dreamed.

farce   a comedy, often with a ridiculous plot which could not possibly be true. (*adjective:* **farcical**)

fiction   a work invented by the writer, with characters and events that are imaginary. Novels, short stories, etc. are all works of fiction. (*adjective:* **fictional**, **fictitious**) **Non-fiction** refers to writing about factual subjects.

fairy tale
or **fairy story**   a popular story usually told to children. These are imaginary stories, often with unreal characters. *Cinderella, Snow White, Mother Goose*, etc. are well-known fairy tales.

foot   a unit of sound in verse, in which there is one stressed syllable, marked /, and one or more unstressed syllables, marked ∪. These are the names for the different kinds of feet:
iamb/iambic ∪ /   trochee/trochaic / ∪
anapest ∪ ∪ /   dactyl / ∪ ∪
spondee / /

free verse   verse in which the lines can vary in length, with no strict metre.

hero/heroine   a) the main character in a book or play, although not necessarily good (see page 45).
b) a good and brave man/woman.
(*adjective:* **heroic**)

heroic couplet   a pair of lines in iambic pentametre (see *metre*) that rhyme.

heroic play   a grand play written in the Restoration period (see page 63).

hexametre   a line of verse with six metrical feet, used by the ancient Greek and Latin poets but not often used in English (see page 103).

**iambic
pentametre**   see *metre*

idiom   an expression or way of saying something that is typical of a language at a certain time. (*adjective:* **idiomatic**)

idyll   a short, descriptive, usually sentimental poem, often with a pastoral theme.

image   a word picture; the putting into words of a sound, sight, smell, taste, etc. by describing it.

imagery   using images such as metaphors (*see*) and similes (*see*) to produce an effect in the reader's imagination (see page 28).

irony   something that has a second meaning intended by the writer, often the opposite, and often with a bitterly humorous tone. In dramatic irony, the audience understands a second meaning that the character does not himself understand. (*adjective:* **ironic**)

legend   a story, usually one that has come down to us from ancient times, so it may not be or seem realistic (see page 17). (*adjective:* **legendary**)

lyric   a) a poem, originally one meant to be sung, which expresses the poet's thoughts and feelings (see page 12). (*adjective:* **lyrical**)
b) *lyrics* is the word now used for the words of a song, especially a pop song.

masque   dramatic entertainment with dancing and music, performed at court and in rich people's houses in the 16th and 17th centuries (see page 50).

melodrama   a play or story in which the events and feelings are deliberately overdone, to be as exciting as possible. (*adjective:* **melodramatic**)

metaphor   a way of describing something by saying that it is like something else, without using the words 'like' or 'as': *e.g. That man is a snake.* Compare *simile*.

metaphysical poetry   the poetry of John Donne and others in the early 17th century (see page 28).

metre   formal rhythm in lines of verse. The verse line is divided into feet which contain different rhythms and stresses (see *foot*). The commonest English metre is the **iambic pentametre**, with five iambs or iambic feet:

e.g. Sŏ lóng | ăs mén | căn bréathe | ŏr éyes | căn see, | Sŏ lóng | livĕs thís, | ănd thís | givĕs lífe | tŏ thée. |

miracle or mystery plays   drama of the late mediaeval times, always with religious subjects (see page 20).

monologue   a speech by one person. **Interior monologue** is the name given to a prose style used by James Joyce and others, which gave the reader the stream of thoughts and feelings passing through a character's mind.

morality plays   drama of the 15th century, using arguments between different values, such as Youth, Death, etc. (see page 21).

narrative   the telling of a story. Novels, short stories, etc. are narratives. The **narrator** is a person who tells a story, in a play or a book written in the 'I' form.

naturalism   trying to be as real as possible, especially in plays. (*adjective:* **naturalistic**)

novel   a book-length story whose characters and events are usually imaginary. A writer of novels is a **novelist**.

ode   a poem, originally to be sung, but now a grand lyric poem often in praise of someone or something (see page 76).

onomatopoeia	using the sounds of words, in poetry, to make the sound of what is being described: *e.g.* the word 'cuckoo' is onomatopoeic, because it is like the sound that the bird makes.
parody	imitating something in such a way as to make the original thing seem ridiculous.
pastoral	style based on an ideal picture of country life, in which the natural world is seen as beautiful and good.
picaresque	style of novels and stories, based on the adventures of men who are often wicked but lovable, and usually including many different places and events (see page 31).
plot	a set of events, or story-line, of a book or a play (see page 39).
preface	an introduction, or short piece of writing that comes before a book or play (see page 167).
prose	written language in its usual form, not in lines of verse (see page 12).
pun	*also* **play on words** an amusing use of a word or phrase that has two meanings, or that sound the same although they are spelt differently.
realism	trying to show life as it really is. (*adjective:* **realistic**)
rhyme	two or more words with the same sound; *e.g.* '*Love*' *and* '*dove*' *are rhymes.* '*Day*' *and* '*weigh*' *rhyme.* '*Meat*' *rhymes with* '*street*'. (see page 8).
rhythm	see *metre*. Metre is the formal rhythm of verse, but prose also has rhythm (see page 38). (*adjective:* **rhythmic**)

romance a love story, or an imaginative story usually with love and adventure. (*adjective:* **romantic**)

Romantic the writers in England between about 1790 and 1830 are known as Romantic poets and authors.

satire a work which tries to show how foolish someone or something is. The writer of satire is a **satirist**. (*verb:* **satirize**; *adjective:* **satirical**) (see page 64).

simile a way of describing something by saying that it is like something else, using the words 'like' or 'as': *e.g. My love is like a red, red rose.* Compare *metaphor.* (see page 31)

sonnet a poem of 14 lines with a fixed form. In the **Petrarchan sonnet** the first eight lines (the *octave*) have a rhyme scheme of *abbaabba* and the next six lines (the *sestet*) rhyme *cdecde.* The **Shakespearean sonnet** is in iambic pentametre and ends with a couplet. The rhymes are *abab cdcd efef gg* or *abba cddc effe gg* (see page 23).

stanza a group of verse lines with a rhyme pattern, such as a *quatrain* (four lines), a *sestet* (six lines), an *octave* (eight lines), etc. (see page 26).

structure the plan of a work, especially a novel or a play, including the plot, the design, etc. (see page 45).

style a way of writing; an author's special way of using language (see page 13).

symbol something that has a deeper meaning or that represents something else: *e.g.* A snake may be a symbol of evil. (*adjective:* **symbolic**)

tragedy something that is very bad or sad. In drama, a tragedy is a serious play, often with an unhappy ending and often concerned with important events (see page 35). (*adjective:* **tragic**)

unity three unities were important in the classical drama – the unities of time, place and action. This meant that the scenes of a play should all take place close to each other, within 24 hours, and should all be about the main story (see page 50).

verse a) a general word for all kinds of poetry. (*no plural*)
b) a single line of poetry. (*plural:* **verses**)
c) a group of lines, a stanza, especially in a song. (*plural:* **verses**)

wit using language in a clever and funny way (see page 59). A **wit** is a person who does this. (*adjective:* **witty**)

Table of historical events

Early Centuries

	7th C.	8th C.	9th C.	10th C.
Historical events	———— The Dark Ages ————	Danish invasions		The Middle Ages
Kings			Alfred	
Writers	Caedmon	Cynewulf	Alfred	Aelfric

Early Centuries

	11th C.	12th C.	13th C.	14th C.	15th C.
Historical events	————The Middle Ages———— **1066** William wins battle of Hastings	**1095-1248** The Crusades	**1215** Magna Carta reduces the king's power	**1348** "The Black Death"	**1431** Joan of Arc burnt **1476** Printing in England **1492** Columbus reaches West Indies **1498** da Gama reaches India by sea
Kings				Edward I, II, III Richard II	Henry IV, V, VI Edward IV, V Richard III Henry VII
Writers			Chaucer	Langland Rolle Wycliffe	Malory
In other countries			Dante Petrarch Boccaccio		Villon

Sixteenth Century	1501-1520	1521-1540
Historical events	**1517** Luther at Wittenburg	**1534** The Church of England separated from Rome
Kings and Queens	⊢ Henry VII ————⊢ ⊢	——— Henry VIII ———
Writers, etc.	⊢ Coverdale —————— ⊢ Tyndale ———— ⊢——— Wyatt ———	
In other countries	⊢Erasmus ———— ⊢——— ⊢Calvin ——— ⊢ Rabelais ——— ⊢ Ariosto ——— ⊢——— Machiavelli ———	⊢Ronsard ——— ⊢Luis de Leon ———

Seventeenth Century	1601-1620	1621-1640
Historical events	**1603** England and Scotland united **1620** The Pilgrim Fathers reach America	**1629** Trouble between Charles I and Parliament
Kings and Queens	Elizabeth I ⊣ ⊢———— James I ———	⊣ ⊢———— Charles I ⊢
Writers, etc.	⊢ Fletcher ——— ⊢——— Herrick ——— ⊢ Jonson ——— ⊢ Shakespeare ———— ⊢ Walton ———	⊢Buckingham ——— ⊢——— Bunyan ⊢Dryden ——— ⊢Etherege ——— ⊢ Evelyn ——— ⊢Locke ——— ⊢Lovelace ——— ⊢Pepys ——— ⊢Milton ———
In other countries	⊢ Cervantes ——— ⊢——— Lope de Vega ——— ⊢ Calderón ——— ⊢——— Descartes ——— ⊢——— Corneille ———	⊢La Fontaine ——— ⊢——— Molière ———

1541-1560	1561-1580	1581-1600
1554 Mary marries Philip of Spain and reintroduces Roman Catholicism	**1577-80** Drake sails round the world	**1588** Spanish Armada

Edward VI — Mary — Elizabeth I

⊢Bacon
⊢Beaumont
⊢Donne
⊢Drayton
⊢Fletcher
⊢Robert Greene
⊢Hakluyt
⊢Herrick
⊢Jonson
⊢Kyd
⊢Lyly
⊢Marlowe
⊢Nash
⊢Raleigh
Sackville
⊢Shakespeare
⊢Sidney
Spenser
⊢Walton
⊢Webster

⊢Cervantes

1641-1660	1661-1680	1681-1700
1642 The Civil War begins **1649** Charles I put to death	**1665** The Great Plague **1666** The Great Fire of London	**1688** James II fails to reintroduce Catholicism. William of Orange invited to England

no king — Charles II — James II — William & Mary

⊢Addison
⊢Congreve
⊢Defoe
⊢Steele
⊢Swift
⊢Vanbrugh
⊢Wycherley

⊢Racine

Eighteenth Century	1701-1720	1721-1740
Historical events	**1702**-13 War of the Spanish Succession **1715** Jacobite rising	
Kings and Queens	⊢——— Anne ———⊣ ⊢—George I ———⊣ ⊢	
Writers, etc.	⊢Congreve——————————— ⊢Defoe—— ⊢Fielding——— ⊢Gray— ⊢Johnson— ⊢Richardson— ⊢Sterne— ⊢Swift— ⊢Thomson—	⊢Burke——— ⊢ Cowper ——— ⊢Goldsmith—— ⊢Smollett——— ⊢Walpole——
In other countries	⊢Voltaire——— ⊢ Rousseau———	

Nineteenth Century	1801-1820	1821-1840
Historical events	**1815** Battle of Waterloo - defeat of Napoleon	**1832** English Reform Act, a first step towards real democracy
Kings and Queens	⊢——— George III———⊣	⊢—George IV——⊣ ⊢Wm. IV—⊣ ⊢
Writers, etc.	⊢Austen——— ⊢Byron— ⊢Carlyle— ⊢Coleridge — ⊢de Quincey— ⊢Dickens— ⊢Gaskell— ⊢Hazlitt— ⊢Keats— ⊢Macaulay— ⊢Poe— ⊢Ruskin— ⊢Scott— ⊢Tennyson— ⊢Thackeray— ⊢Wordsworth—	⊢Brontë, C— Browning, R——— ⊢Butler— ⊢Carroll—— ⊢Eliot— ⊢Rossetti, D G——— ⊢Trollope———
In other countries	⊢Victor Hugo——— ⊢Pushkin———	⊢Tolstoy———

1741-1760	1761-1780	1781-1800
1745 Second Jacobite rising defeated at Culloden **1756-63** Seven Years War - British gains in India and Canada	**1776** Declaration of American Independence	**1789** French Revolution begins **1796** Napoleon's early victories

George II ———————————| |——————————————— George III ———————————

|— Austen ———

—oswell ———————————————————————————————————

|— Blake ————————

|—Burns ————————

|— Chatterton ———————

|—Coleridge————

—ibbon ————————————

|— Scott ————————

|— Sheridan ————————

|—Wordsworth ————————

|—Goethe ————————

|——Schiller ————————

1841-1860	1861-1880	1881-1900
1854-56 Crimean War **1857** Indian Mutiny	**1861-65** American Civil War **1865** Death of Lincoln	**1899-1902** Boer War in South Africa

——————————————— Victoria ———————————

|— Conrad ————————

—ardy ————————————————————

—ater ————————

|—Stevenson ————————

—Swinburne ————————

|— Wilde ————————

—Mark Twain ————————

Twentieth Century	1901-1920	1921-1940	1941-1960	1961-1980
Historical events	**1914-18** World War I **1920** League of Nations	**1929** World slump begins **1939** World War II begins	**1941** Japan enters the war **1945** World War II ends; United Nations **1953** Everest climbed **1957** Sputnik I in space	**1963** Death of President Kennedy **1969** US moon landing **1973** Britain joins EEC; Arab-Israeli war **1978** John Paul II first Polish Pope **1979** US embassy hostages
Kings and Queens	Edward VII —⊣ ⊢—— George V —————⊣ ⊢—		George VI —— ⊢—	———— Elizabeth II ————
Writers, etc.	⊢ Auden ———— ⊢ Beckett ———— Bennett ———— Brooke ———— ⊢ Burgess ———— Compton-Burnett ———— Eliot ———— Galsworthy ———— ⊢ Golding ———— ⊢ Greene, Graham ———— Huxley, Aldous ———— Joyce ———— ⊢ Larkin ———— Lawrence, D H ———— Lawrence, T E ———— ⊢ Lessing ———— Maugham ———— ⊢—— Orwell ———— ⊢ Osborne ———— Owen ———— ⊢ Pinter ———— Priestley ———— Shaw ———— Sitwell, Edith ———— ⊢ Thomas, Dylan ———— ⊢ Waugh, Evelyn ———— Wells ———— ⊢ Wesker ———— Woolf ———— Yeats ————			

Index

Writers named in the book appear in the index with dates of birth and death. Where there is more than one reference, the number in **bold** type shows the page on which the main discussion of the writer's work begins.